JEWISH ENCOUNTERS

Jonathan Rosen, General Editor

Jewish Encounters is a collaboration between Schocken and Nextbook, a project devoted to the promotion of Jewish literature, culture, and ideas.

PUBLISHED

THE LIFE OF DAVID · Robert Pinsky
MAIMONIDES · Sherwin B. Nuland
BARNEY ROSS · Douglas Century
BETRAYING SPINOZA · Rebecca Goldstein
EMMA LAZARUS · Esther Schor
THE WICKED SON · David Mamet
MARC CHAGALL · Jonathan Wilson
JEWS AND POWER · Ruth R. Wisse
BENJAMIN DISRAELI · Adam Kirsch
RESURRECTING HEBREW · Ilan Stavans

FORTHCOMING

The Life of David

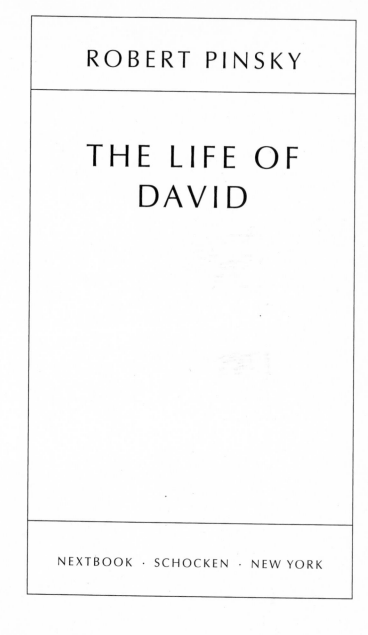

ROBERT PINSKY

THE LIFE OF DAVID

NEXTBOOK · SCHOCKEN · NEW YORK

Copyright © 2005 by Robert Pinsky
All rights reserved. Published in the United States by
Schocken Books, a division of Random House, Inc., New York,
and in Canada by Random House of Canada Limited, Toronto.

Schocken and colophon are registered trademarks of
Random House, Inc.

Originally published in hardcover by Schocken Books,
a division of Random House, Inc., New York, in 2005.

Library of Congress Cataloging-in-Publication Data
Pinsky, Robert.
    The life of David / Robert Pinsky.
        p.   cm. — (Jewish encounters)
    ISBN 978-0-8052-1153-5
    1. David, King of Israel. 2. Israel—Kings and rulers—
Biography. 3. Bible. O.T.—Biography. I. Title. II. Series.
                BS580.D3P56 2005
                222'.4092—dc22
                                    2005041696

www.schocken.com

Printed in the United States of America
First Paperback Edition
2   4   6   8   9   7   5   3

CONTENTS

ACKNOWLEDGMENTS

Friends have helped me immensely with their suggestions and encouragement: Frank Bidart, Alfred Corn, David Ferry, Louise Glück, Stephen Greenblatt, Robert Hass, Gail Mazur, Michael Mazur, Ellen Pinsky, Nicole Pinsky, Tom Sleigh, Harry Thomas, C. K. Williams.

When I directed some queries to Professor James Kugel, whom I do not know personally, he responded generously and promptly.

In Jonathan Rosen I have had a blessedly exceptional editor—a writer whose judgment and knowledge challenged me beyond what I could have done without him. Phrases of his have found their way into my sentences, and his critical imagination informs every part of this book.

Among the books that have guided me, I am especially grateful to two masterworks: Louis Ginzberg's mighty *Legends of the Jews* and Hayyim Bialik's artful *And It Came to Pass*. I have also benefited from the scholarship and insight of Robert Alter's modern translation and notes, in his *The David Story*, and similarly from Everett Fox's *Give Us a King!: Samuel, Saul, and David*. The magisterial *Early History of Israel* by Roland de Vaux helped me try to envision the lives of biblical Hebrews. I relied on Rabbi Samson Raphael Hirsch's

Acknowledgments

classic 1882 *The Psalms: Translation and Commentary*, rendered into English from Hirsch's German by Gertrude Hirschler. I thank these writers, and the countless masters before them, for my good fortune in trying to balance my imagination on their shoulders.

The Life of David

I

David

Of the Thousand Great Stories, more than a few are about him. David and Goliath and David and Bathsheba of course, but also David and Saul, David and Jonathan, David and Absalom. Tales of battle, of sex, of the uncanny, of needy mistrust between the generations, of loyalty and betrayal, politics, incest. David and Amnon, David and the Witch of Endor, David and Abigail. The great neglected story of love and undying hate between a man and a woman, David and Michal. David and the doomed generals out of a Shakespeare history play, Abner and Joab. David and the crippled son of Saul, Mephibosheth. David and Abishag. And the implicit story of the remorseless wheel of time, David and Solomon.

He is wily like Odysseus and an impetuous daredevil like the Scarlet Pimpernel. Like Hamlet, he pretends to be crazy. Like Joan of Arc, he comes from nowhere, ardent and innocent, to infuriate the conventional elders. Like the Athenian rogue Alcibiades he goes over to the enemy side for a time. Like Robin Hood, he gathers a band of outcasts and outlaws in the wilderness. Like Lear, he is overthrown and betrayed by his offspring. Like Tristan and Cyrano, he masters the harp as well as the sword: a poet as well as a warrior-killer, but as a poet he is far above any other hero, and as a killer no one among the poets can even approach him.

He must have actually existed, and most of it must be true, writes the upper-class Englishman Duff Cooper, because no people would deliberately invent a national hero so deeply flawed. The flaws of Lancelot make that adulterer a more heroic knight than Galahad the chosen of God: David is both, flawed and chosen, as in the span of his life he is both the golden lad and the grizzled adulterer. The adultery exacerbated (or depending on perspective ameliorated or mystified) by the fact that as the prophet Nathan points out to him he already had wives and sub-wives by the dozen.

We love our heroes at a level beyond reason, an intuitive plane where our shared feelings are tribal and nearly animal, rather than legalistic: as unheeding of priests and lawyers, though intimidated by them, in our collective public fascination with the hero as we are in our individual, private love life.

A hero is one who does great deeds and suffers for the good of a community, but in addition the hero must be talked about. "Unsung hero" is a paradox. The deeds and suffering become heroic as we tell stories about them. So that anthropological figure of action needs the other figure who sings, who tells the stories. For the hero to be celebrated requires the artist who imagines the celebration: David the warrior-artist is both. He is the most manifold and various of heroes. His name is thought to have meant "beloved."

His world is a realm of multiple tribes. More than piety might like, the Jewish and non-Jewish designations blur: Ephraimites, Amalekites, Benjamites, Maachathites, Harodites, Gileadites, Zebulunites, Carmelites, Pherethites, Ammonites. From the Zidonians, Solomon the Wise in his old age contracted worship of Ashtoreth, the abomination—more gently known as the love goddess called Astarte by the Greeks and Ishtar by the Babylonians. A deity of fruitfulness as well as beauty. Her followers among the ancient Jewish tribes left a little stone image of her that survives with other ancient artifacts among the much later six-pointed stars and the seven-branched candlesticks in the Jewish museum in Los Angeles: the lady Astarte who embodies some of the attributes of Solomon's mother Bathsheba. Astarte or Ishtar is echoed in the name of the Jewish heroine Esther, who in the weave of syllables and legends became the consort of King Ahasuerus, which is to say the Persian ruler Xerxes I.

As the bloodline tangle of tribes indicates a world of overlapping shadows and smoky alliances, geographic notions too must be imagined as shifting, each place with its countless layers of demarcation and language. The deceptive familiarity of place-names adapted into English—Shiloh, Gilead, Gaza, Bethel—should be balanced by less assimilated names: the Wilderness of Ziph, Ashdod, the City of Dagon, Helam, Nob, Kirjath-Jearim, Shalisha, Ziklag.

Immediate as a dream, in a setting as remote as the planets of science fiction, David's career with its temporary victories and enduring glories, its obdurate calculus of pain, plays out a fundamental drama of all life. Overlaid by a system of rewarded piety and punished defection, a system embodied by the prophet Samuel, David's drama enacts forces of ambition and destruction, love and betrayal, volcanic strivings and appetite. The story manifests an undying wonderment at the spectacle of a beautiful boy who pursues his course and flourishes as a dominant hero, and then becomes an anguished old man.

That relatively secular story, the story of King David's career, was written probably in the time of Solomon (the tenth century B.C.E.)—that is, a generation or two after the events—by the author scholars have called the Early Source. The Late Source, compiled and edited hundreds of years later, adds what I have called the overlay of divine punishment and reward, including Samuel's strange and eloquent warning to the people about the nature of monarchy ("This will be the manner of the king that shall reign over you"). The Early Source tells virtually all of 2 Samuel, the account of David's kingship and the destiny of the people of Israel; the Late Source tells the life of Samuel in 1 Samuel, and contributes the narratives of how God's punishment deals with Saul and before him with the corrupt and idol-worshipping sons of the prophet Eli.

The Early Source is largely a nationalistic hero narrative. The Late Source is largely a religious moral narrative. Still later editing and interpolations imposed by a Deuteronomist or committee of Deuteronomists further emphasized the principle of obedience to God. Other scholars have seen pro-Saul and pro-David sources. The frayed narratives, the peculiar knots, the clashes and oppositions, even the narrative contradictions of these strands do not produce mere incoherence. Rather, in the way of texts that have formed us for centuries, the meldings and inconsistencies of competing voices make the text read the reader all the more deeply. Because the Late Source tries to pull the story away from the monarchy and toward theological meanings, the career of David becomes an even more urgent, enigmatic account of destiny and freedom. Because it has been made to issue from the opposed story of Samuel (and Samuel's interpretation of the story of Saul), the story of David is all the more magnetic, tormented and glorious.

With its emphasis on competition and succession, loyalty and rivalry among men and between sons and fathers, it seems a male story, in the primal way of ironbound tradition; yet women play powerful roles. Michal, Abigail, Bathsheba, make decisions that determine outcomes. The matrilinear chains, counter-tune to the male begettings, manifest the way all stories, in fact all people, owe their being to origins multiple and unknown, a tangle of forgotten roots. The Moabites (and thus David) are said to descend from the cave where the daughters of Lot got their father drunk and tricked him into lying with them—like some scandalous story from Ovid or an Inuit origin myth. As an Ephrathite, David belongs to the one tribal group named from the matrilinear line: Ephrath was the wife of Caleb, great-grandson of the tribal patriarch Judah. The stories of the girl Abishag, the matriarch Ruth, the wives Bathsheba and Michal, gesture toward mythologies and histories and psychological imperatives beyond the masculine tribal system as they are outside the later theologies. What covert or defiant hunger harbored that image of Astarte?

Or is the story of Lot and his daughters an ancient, mischievous insult, a Hebrew invention to taunt the Moabites— with the Hebrew David's descent from Moab a forgotten or unanticipated twist? Or an added layer? A braiding-together of cultures or a cleaving-apart? These are the histories earlier than the Early Source, and more fundamental: the infinite regress of obscured Sources behind everything that survives. Subterranean fires and currents, forming the stories that form us, make themselves visible in the career of the hero.

II

Cousin Goliath

David of Judah, the eighth and youngest son of Jesse the Bethlehemite, is descended not only from Israelites but also from Moabites, through his great-grandmother Ruth.

We fumble to understand that fact in our own terms. How alien were the Moabites, those worshippers of Chemosh and descendants of the right-doing though incestuous gentile Lot? How different was their speech from that of the Israelites? What would the sound of a Moabite name be like? Is "Goliath" a Moabite name? Is "Ruth"?

What were David and Goliath to one another? Enemies of course. Foreigners. Also, familiar to one another and even, it has been proposed, relatives. Even here with his legendary enemy, the story of David involves the mysteries of how a person belongs or does not belong with another, or with a family or a tribe or a people. The youngest brother or sister is a staple figure in folktales possibly for this reason: the runt or underdog is also the least important in primogeniture, the most distant from the rootstock.

And in the traditional way of the old tales in so many cultures, David's brothers can be cruel toward him, judgmental beyond mockery. Jesse sends David to the battle camp with some food for the brothers, bread and grain and also ten cheeses for their captain. The brothers overhear David asking about Goliath's challenge to the Hebrew army, apparently in a tone they don't like.

Eliab the eldest brother says to the boy: "Why have you come down? And with whom have you left those few sheep in the wilderness? I know your presumption, and the evil of your heart; for you have come down to see the battle."

"What have I done now?" says David. (In English, the Revised Standard is sometimes best for dialogue, however much the King James excels for poetry.) "Was it not but a word?"

Here is the contention between brothers, savage yet all but comically familiar. The contest with Goliath is foreshadowed by the contest with Eliab. And just as the courthouse rarely records the birth of a modern baby called Goliath, we tend equally to neglect the name Eliab. We may neglect it even more—many zoo creatures, and even pets, have been called Goliath, but not Eliab.

And yet the name is common enough in Israel, the syllables of the older brother's name defiantly alive against odds, like the language in which it means something like "My-God-My-Father"—with that meaning too, seeming more appropriate when applied to the Lord's favorite, the beloved and effortlessly supplanting David.

When God sends the prophet Samuel to the house of

Jesse for the purpose of anointing one of the brothers, the prophet notices Eliab at once:

"When they came, he looked on Eliab and thought, Surely the Lord's anointed is before him." This recalls Samuel identifying the first king, when the strapping, handsome young country boy Saul stood above all others "from his shoulders and upward." Like Saul, Eliab by his stature and bearing stands out, as in the literal, root sense of the old expression "head and shoulders."

But no, Eliab is not the one. In the obscurity of his name, this eldest brother is more thoroughly defeated by David, sent into a deeper unredeemed oblivion, than is Goliath. The second-to-eldest brother comes in to be scrutinized by Samuel: Abinadab. "Neither has the Lord chosen this one." And so too Shamah, and all seven of the elder brothers, before the handsome and ruddy youngster, with his "beautiful eyes," is recalled from where he has been watching over the sheep.

The really powerful stories don't always need to make sense—the mess of *Hamlet*, the impossible hash of *Lear*, or less loftily the tangled screenplay of *The Big Sleep*, with its extra murder that the original book's author Raymond Chandler himself couldn't explain. It is even expressive that the scene of the boy who delivers cheese and loaves to the encampment and the scene where Samuel looks over the brothers sit awkwardly in any chronology: if David has been anointed, why do neither he nor any of the brothers seem to recall the fact? The seams that show between the pieces of narrative, the bits apparently soldered in from the Late

Source—only emphasize the nature of the events: urgent and ungovernable as dreamlife.

So David—who has already become King Saul's harp-player, his voice in song driving away the evil spirit in Saul; and then has become the king's shield-bearer, allowed by Jesse to remain with the king at Saul's courtly request—somehow this David is again the shepherd boy, sent by his father to deliver cheeses. David defeats Eliab and Abinadab and Shamah and he defeats Goliath and indeed he defeats Saul. All at once, in a sense. In the fractured and not perfectly logical sequence of 1 Samuel, David's familial conquests over his intimates echo his victories in battle, and the victories in battle in turn echo the way he overcomes his brothers and bests the patriarchal figure of his king. In the blurred chronology no enactment has flawless primacy—which gives the telling not less but greater force, amplified by the irrational. The essential combats of David are intimate, otherworldly and ongoing.

Eliab, Abinadab, Shamah: the stress on the second syllable in all these names, I think, as also in "Goliath." Here again, as with "Shiloh" compared with "Kirjath-Jearim," a misleading familiarity might lull the American reader: David and his great-grandmother Ruth and her mother-in-law Naomi and his father Jesse sound like people we meet at a wedding. Whereas the names of these brothers are more alien to our ears (though I have met a Shamah) than that of Goliath. Going back three generations, the sister of Ruth was the barbaric-sounding Orpah. (Almost impossible to keep the brain from familiarizing it to "Oprah.") We should not try to imagine the feelings of Shocoh and Barzillai the Meholathite and Mephibosheth the son of Saul and David's comrade Eleazar the son of Dodo the Ahohite more quickly than we can pronounce their names. To those personages, was any of these sounds more exotic than another? ("Mephibosheth" is a scribal compromise, substituted for an actual name even more bizarre.) Abinadab and Dodo are not simply our relatives in biblical dress, any more than they are Gregory Peck or Richard Gere in robe and sandals, speaking stilted English or subtitled Hebrew to indicate their biblical condition. They are Jews, but in significant ways they are more like Bedouins than someone from Great Neck. We may read them in Elizabethan or Jacobean English, but they are not seventeenth-century gentlemen and ladies. The quality of the foreign, like the strangeness of the exile, is to be respected.

Ruth, the archetypal outsider amid the alien corn, embodies that foreign quality. The sources of these now bookbound clashes and treaties, rapes and feasts, betrayals and sacrifices, unfolded under a different sky, where tremendous voltages of xenophobic or incestuous or fratricidal passion flash between the alien and the intimate. In that other world, sometimes even more rapidly than in the one we know, what was alien becomes familial, or the familial becomes alienated. When family or tribe become treacherous, sometimes the enemy tents provide shelter. David brings his parents to the king of Moab, for safety from Saul's rages. He serves the Philistine ruler Achish, King of Gath, as bodyguard and trusted lieutenant, for over a year.

This is one meaning of the folktale of the Clever Younger Son: the conventional hierarchies and bonds are imperfect. Repeatedly, the order of things must be supplanted by guts or brains, in the interest of survival. That dark, primitive thread of necessary violation runs through the elaborate tapestry of David's career: a tragedy of the dynasty-founder, self-made and self-ruined and self-made anew. The underdog boy and the calculating ruler share an unending struggle.

With what goal, precisely? To make a secure place for oneself? To gain an enduring name? To serve the people? Or God? To establish the survival of the Jews? These biblical narratives of identity, components of the story of a people that miraculously endures, tend to be narratives of exile from Genesis onward: our life on this earth begins with expulsion and fratricide. The intensity of the xenophobia is matched by a ferocious apprehension of the family as a node of conflict and treachery: Joseph sold into slavery by his brothers; Esau dispossessed by his brother; Ishmael expelled; Moses at Sinai betrayed by his people and his brother, and at Pisgah interdicted from the Promised Land. In the family as in war, the hero struggles for a secure place. That ultimately tragic pursuit—there seems to be no such place, or only in promise—underlies David's story as it does the stories of the spurned son Ishmael and the dispossessed brother Esau, the adopted exile Joseph and the adopted princely child Moses.

It is a commonplace to mock the exhausting chains of "begats." We skip over them, but they are full of choral meaning. Those generational landslides of consonant and barbarous vowel, treasured and denominating links in the miraculous, much-desired chain of connection, remind us that this is no more the world of Uncle Saul dancing with Aunt Naomi than Abraham is Lincoln, or Ahab is a whaling man. To require these genealogical accounts is to recognize that human connections are fragile.

Or in another way, the obsessive biblical rehearsing of genealogies and place-names do indeed recall the world of our aunts and uncles, presidents and demented sea captains. The chant of recognition winding through the generations, binding people (and sometimes places), gives a fundamental comfort, even a measure of reconciliation to mortality, met with a matrix of generations and origins, the web of relation—the familiar.

Ruth and her sister Orpah were daughters of Eglon, King of Moab, says the twentieth-century Hebrew poet Hayyim Nahman Bialik, and according to the "Scroll of Orpah," says Bialik, both princesses were great beauties. But Orpah was noisy and unruly like a young camel, while Ruth was mild and shy as a doe. Their father King Eglon was a bull-like, thriving man who "worshipped his god Chemosh in joy and gladness." Eglon dealt harshly with his neighbors, the children of Israel. Yet at the same time Eglon feared the Israelites' God, and treated His name respectfully, even while he oppressed and tormented the Hebrew people. Such, in Bialik's telling (which improvises on Talmudic lore), is the royal father of Ruth and Orpah.

King Eglon's prudent respect for the God of the Israelites leads him to allow the marriage of his princess daughters to Chilion and Mahlon, sons of the immigrant widow Naomi. Chilion and Mahlon soon die, perhaps sickly like their father before them, who was driven to Moab by a famine in Judea—the desperation, failure and sickness that shadow all stories of immigrant survival. And the Hebrew widow Naomi bereft now of sons too will return to Judea. Naomi says farewell to her daughters-in-law, Ruth and Orpah:

"Go, return to the house of your mother, and may the Lord deal kindly with you as you have dealt with the dead and with me."

In what seems possibly a ritual or maybe even a legal formality, these daughters-in-law both offer to return with Naomi to her people and leave their native land of Moab. But the older woman tells them, "Turn again, my daughters, go your way." And they lift up their voices and weep, and Orpah kisses her mother-in-law goodbye; but Ruth makes her great declaration:

"Entreat me not to leave thee, or to return from following after thee. For whither thou goest, I will go; and where thou lodgest, I will lodge. Thy people will be my people, and thy God my God. Where thou diest, I will die, and there will I be buried."

So hearing these words that reach to some source of attachment or destiny maybe deeper than mere Eros, Naomi returns from Moab to her people accompanied by her widowed daughter-in-law Ruth. Meanwhile the other daughter-in-law, Orpah with the manners of a young camel, in Bialik's telling returns to her life of a Moabite princess, in her own mother's house.

And it came to pass that a Philistine came through Moab, a tremendous man in military dress, bearing weapons all over his body, a descendant of the prehistoric giants. And seeing this glorious figure, Orpah in Bialik's words "joined herself to him." A tall man's man, we can imagine, as striking as Eliab when he walks into his father's house and Samuel thinks for a moment, *Here is the one.* As to Orpah: "And, as a dog followeth after his master, so she followed after her Philistine lover to his own place, the city of Gath."

And to Boaz her second husband Ruth bore Obed. And Obed begat Jesse and Jesse begat David. While meanwhile, in Gath too the begetting proceeded through the generations to the grandson of Orpah. He was six cubits and a span tall, that is six times the distance from a man's elbow (Latin *cubitum*) to the fingertips. His armor coat of chain mail weighed five thousand shekels, or well over a hundred pounds. He wore brass greaves on his legs and a sword hung at his waist. His spear was like a weaver's beam and in the field of war his shield-bearer stood with him.

So the youngest son who had been scolded and challenged by his brothers and disregarded them went out with his sling to defeat his gigantic cousin, contrary to the evident hierarchies of strength and primogeniture. Their challenges to one another have a formal quality, an implicit shared protocol of threat and boast. Goliath of Gath says to David of Bethlehem:

"Come to me, and I will give thy flesh unto the fowls of the air, and to the beasts of the field."

David says to the Philistine, "Thou comest to me with a

sword, and with a spear, and with a shield: but I come to thee in the name of the Lord of hosts, the God of the armies of Israel, whom thou hast defied. This day will the Lord deliver thee into mine hand; and I will smite thee, and take thy head from thee: and I will give the carcasses of the host of the Philistines this day unto the fowls of the air, and to the wild beasts of the earth; that all the earth may know that there is a God in Israel."

The story has the power of what is clearly legendary but could have happened: even a warrior who stands a bit over six cubits is not an impossibility. And as what could have happened has certain overtones not achieved by what did happen or did not happen, the varying scale of the narrative, its shifting perspective, its warped chronologies and conflicted meanings, all help make it indelible.

So it is with our misconception of David's sling as childish, something first laughed at by the opposing troops as a toy, then amazing them when it proves lethal. We can retain that fabricated, modern meaning along with the reality: that the sling was a fearsome infantry weapon for centuries, mentioned by Herodotus and Thucydides—as well as in Judges, where the seven hundred chosen left-handed slingers of Benjamin "could sling stones at an hair breadth, and not miss." The slinger was more mobile than the archer, and with a greater accurate range, some say with a more damaging projectile. The Romans had medical tongs designed specifically for removing the stones or lead bullets shot by sling to penetrate a soldier's body, as David's stone penetrated the skull of Goliath.

Before that fatal encounter with Goliath comes another confrontation, between David and King Saul. In Saul's royal tent, the delivery boy David, who has outraged his brother by asking self-confident questions, and who will outboast Goliath, speaks his confidence to the king, too, saying of Goliath, "let no man's heart fail because of him; thy servant will go and fight with this Philistine."

And Saul: "Thou art not able to go against this Philistine to fight with him: for thou art but a youth, and he a man of war from his youth."

David's answer here in Saul's tent, before the fight, perhaps foreshadows in its detailed self-assurance Saul's angry humiliation when he will soon hear the dancing women chant, "Saul hath slain his thousands, and David his ten thousands."

David says to Saul, in the tent, "Thy servant kept his father's sheep, and there came a lion, and a bear, and took a lamb out of the flock, and I went out after him, and smote him, and delivered it out of his mouth. And when he rose against me, I caught him by his beard, and smote him, and slew him. Thy servant slew both the lion and the bear. And this uncircumcised Philistine shall be as one of them, seeing he hath defied the armies of the living God."

The respectful formula of "thy servant" authorizes the naked assertion of prowess. Fluent, fluid, David who runs at Goliath—like a point guard ready to flick the basketball here or there—might be maddeningly quick of speech and thought and foot for the larger men: an agile shape-shifter. The sudden astonishment when David sprints forward must have frozen Goliath, making him a better target. Saul who stands head and shoulders above other men, and big Eliab who reminds Samuel of Saul, might feel some sympathy for the giant immobilized in his armor. When Saul in a paranoid rage hurls a spear at David, who ducks it, the king has a tellingly specific image in mind: "And Saul sought to smite David even to the wall with the javelin"—that is, to pin him down. To fix that quick, assured and well-spoken figure, that articulate dodger, to the wall.

But in the tent David's quickness moves the king. The shepherd's confidence persuades him. An intimate, familial feeling comes from the next, brilliantly imagined scene. Saul puts his own armor onto David, and places a brass helmet on the boy's head: the coziness of shared garments and hand-me-downs, along with the symbolism of supplantation, even a kind of crowning. The Early Source, a writer of the greatest imagination, lets those emotional currents, warm and chilly, continue and flow into a charming, comic moment: weighted down with armor, helmet, sword, the youth "assayed to go" but finds that, as David says, "I cannot go with these; for I have not proved them": in Robert Alter's modern translation: "he was unable to walk, for he was unused to it."

So he takes off the heavy armor and goes out, and with a smooth river stone and a snap of his limber sling David, limber and smooth himself, defeats the giant. He cuts the tall opponent to size, the great armored body of his cousin sprawled facedown, possibly still twitching. With Goliath's own sword he strikes at Goliath's neck and cuts off the head. Using Goliath's blade to despatch Goliath is like David in its lethal, pragmatic wit. Niccolò Machiavelli celebrates David's refusal of Saul's armor as a demonstration that "the arms of others either fall from your back, or they weigh you down, or they bind you fast." By using his enemy's weapon against him, David goes beyond that mere prudence. As the stone in the forehead makes grotesquely literal the force of a superior intelligence over a lesser one, so beheading Goliath with his own sword makes literal and actual David's ability to exploit whatever he finds at hand—including the supposed assets of his opponent.

Then David is conducted by Abner, the great general of the army, into the tent of King Saul where David presents Saul with the head of the Philistine. The harper whose music drove the evil spirit from the king has defeated the enemy champion. Abner the general, the mighty henchman or executive officer, a category of man always ready to take power if the king's successor heirs prove weak, would have the standard man of power's attitude toward poetry and harp-playing. Saul at least would be aware of the therapeutic effect of David's art. But neither man would likely be at that stage of life where a man of power, developing spiritual hungers, turns toward religion or poetry or in our contemporary life a twelve-step program. So neither man necessarily would consciously think outright, *Someday this one will write my death-lament.* But aware mainly of David's surprising victory, they might each have had a presentiment about his eloquence, or his sheer infuriating grace, the quick elegiac ivy of art that attaches itself to stone or to living limbs, and beautifies and outlasts them. David who defeats and survives brother Eliab and cousin Goliath will outlast Saul and Abner, and about those two doomed paternal elders he will compose great funereal poems.

Abner conducts David carrying the freshly severed head into the tent of the king. And in the fractured dream-logic of the spliced narrative, Saul as if blinking or in a trance, almost like Lear waking from his madness and staring at Cordelia, says to him:

"Whose son art thou, thou young man?"

And David answers,

"I am the son of thy servant Jesse the Bethlehemite."

III

The King's
Other Daughter

They were polygamists, those monotheists.

That knowledge affects the scene when the king offers David his daughter in marriage: the formula that ends many of the Northern fairy tales, coming here near the outset of the young man's adventures.

As in the fairy tales, the young man is a nobody who has unexpectedly triumphed against the odds. He is a sheepherder, and even within the undistinguished family of Jesse a delivery boy. Some legends say he was old Jesse's son by a slave girl. The young man would have to recognize the generosity of the offer, appreciate it even though both of them knew that a king might have dozens of daughters by various wives and concubines, just as they both knew that this particular king himself too had been born a nobody. Saul had come to the title by a process of halfhearted ceremony determined more by the wills and imaginations of other people than by any action or words of his own.

The people wanted a king, and Samuel the anointing

prophet who warned them against kings chose Saul, who hid in the baggage in an attempt to avoid it. And Samuel wrote down the rights and duties of the kingship and that was that. "But some worthless fellows said, How can this man save us? And they despised him, and brought him no presents. But he held his peace." And before the choosing, before the anointing that hadn't proved much, when he was the young harp-plucking shepherd's age, he had been neither a king nor an astounding youth, but just Saul.

Big, good-looking Saul. It was no gangster story of making himself king by grabbing power, shouldering others aside, crushing or subverting or outright assassinating his rivals. Yet the prophet Samuel read God's will accurately in choosing Saul. His capacity to lead, his ruthlessness, his willingness to murder and lie and extort in the name of policy, the art of playing courtiers and colleagues one against the other, all were doubtless rooted more firmly in Saul for being not inborn, as they might be for some prince born to intrigues and courtly assassinations. With no such inheritance Saul had to study kingship painstakingly like a trade, mastered over decades as he consolidated his growing hoard of power. So he shaped his native capacities for cunning and violence, his intimidating physical presence, into tools of the rank he never sought. He could be guided only by his own desperation and intelligence. The man who had selected him and anointed him was against the very idea of him. Then that same man, Samuel, would seize an occasion of failed protocol to inform Saul that the Lord was sorry he had been made king. And Saul begged pardon, and pardon was refused. No wonder his mind became prey to evil spirits from God.

David in an opposite way comes to eminence with one spectacular performance: his first recognition and his first victory are simultaneous. He does not so much rise as appear, whereas Saul, though big and good-looking, comes to office before he has proved himself. At his first, dire crisis of leadership, he must deal with terrible threats from the enemy and anguished disarray among his people. Single combat will not do: he must rally the children of Israel, who except for a handful have despised the untested king, and sent him no gifts. Saul knows his subjects:

"And the spirit of God came upon Saul when he heard those tidings, and his anger was kindled greatly. And he took a yoke of oxen and hewed them in pieces, and sent them throughout all the coasts of Israel by the hands of messengers, saying, Whosoever cometh not forth after Saul and after Samuel, so shall it be done unto his oxen. And the fear of the Lord fell on the people, and they came out with one consent."

Thus does young Saul, the first king of the Hebrew people, assemble the great army that defeats the Ammonites, slaying them from early morning into the heat of the day, until the enemy army scatters so that no two of them are left together.

Being king wasn't Saul's idea, it wasn't even exactly the idea of the sour prophet Samuel who anointed him. It was the people's idea, or rather the reverse: it was an idea that came to possess them. They wanted a king, and Saul was the tall specimen who as anybody could see was available—and as the exasperated, unwilling old prophet with his expression of having eaten something bad could see, was eligible. So Saul's accession was less that mobster drama than a tormented version of the ordinary story of some able youth who drifts into a trade and finds himself making a life of it, developing the calluses and specialized muscles, the deformities of body and soul peculiar to that one occupation, while he makes a living and grows old in it.

It wasn't an ambitious gangster rise, but his first decisive action was gangsterish. The cutting to pieces of the oxen, and sending the still-bloody pieces to all parts of the country with their unmistakable message of Saul's ruthless resolve, almost precluded the need for anyone to consider the threat—because the actual threat was preempted, a kind of detail, compared to the matter-of-fact savagery of the information: *I will do anything I need to.*

The violent clarity of that notification, at once symbolic and literal, is like something from the *Godfather* movies or *The Sopranos*, those fantasies of ruthless patriarchal authority.

And there's a gangsterish quality also in their conversation when the king offers his daughter's hand in marriage to David:

"And Saul said to David, Behold my elder daughter Merab, her will I give thee to wife: only be thou valiant for me, and fight the Lord's battles. For Saul said"—as David will say years later about the husband of a woman he desires— "Let not mine hand be upon him, but let the hand of the Philistines be upon him."

In the movie they might be two elegant hoodlums sitting over drinks on a terrace in black tie, cigars glowing in the dusk. The older man offers his firstborn daughter, smiling, and thinking inwardly that the enemy would likely kill this dangerous young interloper. *"Only be you valiant for me."*

With equal cunning and faked candor, decorously, the young man says that the honor of such a marriage is too great for a man like himself, from a humble family. They are paying one another the compliment of an elaborately feigned respect, as formal and transitory and nearly as impersonal as floral arrangements:

"And David said unto Saul, Who am I? and what is my life, or my father's family in Israel, that I should be son in law to the king?"

A marriage gift to the bride's family is involved. Again one can picture them drawling over their cigars, generously, pretending not to bargain—in a leisurely comradeship, though part of the conversation as reported in the actual text is by messenger, another form of courtly duplicity.

"And David said, Seemeth it to you a light thing to be a king's son in law, seeing that I am a poor man, and lightly esteemed?"

"And Saul said, Thus shall ye say to David. The king desireth not any dowry, but an hundred foreskins of the Philistines, to be avenged of the king's enemies. But Saul thought to make David fall by the hand of the Philistines."

That is, Saul hopes to have David killed and David hopes to avoid the expenses and risks of the marriage, and probably both know neither is deceived. Merab, Saul's elder daughter, does not speak or appear. In the midst of all this masculine, ceremonious falsehood and negotiation, an extraordinary new character enters the story:

"But it came to pass at the time when Merab Saul's daughter should have been given to David, that she was given unto Adriel the Meholathite to wife. And Michal Saul's daughter loved David: and they told Saul and the thing pleased him." Where did Adriel come from? And Michal? The understatement, the absence of explanation, are nearly as thrilling as the information itself.

Michal is the second daughter, a redoubling of the feminist expression "the second sex." And how strikingly she becomes second here!—it *comes to pass*, as simple as that, that Merab *was given to* Adriel the Meholathite. We don't know if this matter of Merab's marriage, disrespectful of David, was deliberately so, or a matter of foreign-policy needs or a superb financial offer—or even actual passion between the couple.

And the passion is possible: not in contemporary terms, not that Adriel was on his Spring Break from Dartmouth and met Merab at a party, not the manners of courtly love as William Shakespeare learned them from Sir Philip Sidney's imitations of Petrarch—but something. Something more ancient, more Eastern and Southern than those models, but passion—and that it is possible is there in the verse immediately after the sudden giving of Merab. Merab is given. In the telling if not in her actual courtship Merab is passive: but *Michal Saul's daughter loved David*. Actively, and adding a new element to our notion of a daughter as submissive chattel, Michal loved David.

And Saul in effect says to the young man, Look here, I will not ask some exorbitant bride-price. Let me deal easily with you, you are a splendid young man: forget the fancy presents, let me save you money—just bring me the foreskins of a hundred Philistines. Meaning, more or less explicitly but with the courtly manners of one who rules, "I want you to die." But also, "I want no blame for it."

And David, with his rosy cheeks and beautiful eyes, as if blowing smoke into the mild night air, at once welcomes and scorns his father-in-law's move by doubling the bet: if you would like the foreskins of a hundred Philistines, I will meet and outdo your lethal generosity by bringing you the foreskins of two hundred Philistines.

"Wherefore David arose and went, he and his men, and slew of the Philistines two hundred men, and David brought their foreskins, and they gave them in full tale to the king, that he might be the king's son in law. And Saul gave him Michal his daughter to wife."

This is the first stage of a great love story that ends with equally great hatred—a story eloquent and enigmatic, and a true marriage worthy of the horrible and compelling image that endorses, even sanctifies it. Hard enough to imagine the grisly bundle of foreskins, a butcher's package, and perhaps more difficult still to envision the harvesting from those corpses, for the fastidious modern reader who may never have seen so much as a chicken killed. Synthetically toughened by the Technicolor special effects of combat or horror movies, can we visualize so many pounds of flesh severed from the flaccid bodies of the dead? Was it a compliment to the bride? A foreshadowing of her stormy, thwarted life?

David will have other wives, many of them, and other women. And Michal will have another husband. But Michal and David are knit together as they are pulled apart by that first symbol of the foreskins, a mutilation that is also a kind of absorption, even an embrace. For unlike scalps or ears, the removed foreskins are not merely enumerative trophies or mutilations: they also make the Philistines more like the Jews, a transformation as uneasy and ambiguous as what may bind a woman to a man.

Or, considering the equipment and dispositions of the actual soldiers who did the gathering, is the word "foreskins" a metonymy, and is what they performed on those corpses more likely not a circumcision but an amputation?—which would change the nature of the tribute to Michal.

Michal the second daughter: her story is not as well known as that of Bathsheba—Michal is second in that too—perhaps because Bathsheba's story is simpler, Michal's stranger and more tortuous, though also perhaps more recognizably close to home.

"And Saul saw and knew that the Lord was with David, and that Michal Saul's daughter loved him. And Saul was yet the more afraid of David; and Saul became David's enemy continually."

Yes and no: continually, yet not continually. In the jagged, imperfect telling and in the events told, Saul and David are alienated and reconciled and murderously alienated again—murderous on Saul's side, but not David's. The younger man puts himself repeatedly in the right. In an incident that is told twice with two different sets of detail, David stealthily takes evidence from an unaware Saul that he has spared him: the spear and water jar sneaked from next to the king's bed while he sleeps (1 Samuel 26:10–25, attributed to the Early Source); a piece cut stealthily from his garment while he urinates (1 Samuel 24:1–22, Late Source). Then David presents the evidence to Saul—"Behold, I spared you." And Saul repents: "You are more righteous than I. I will do you no more harm." But the cycle keeps recurring, suspicion and forbearance and murderous intent, lurching on the contorted axle of Saul's brooding, his terrified rage at the quicksilver, evasive and invincible David who attracts the love of Michal.

And for Saul that love must have been the lighter, the easier to take, the less maddening, of two defections in his own family. Michal after all is the second, and the second most important, of Saul's children to love the harp-player whose very name signifies "He who is loved." Saul's son Jonathan also loves David, perhaps sexually:

"The soul of Jonathan was knit with the soul of David, and Jonathan loved him as his own soul." And as a marriage is a contract sealed by a ceremony, this binding-together, too: "Then Jonathan and David made a covenant, because he loved him as his own soul. And Jonathan stripped himself of the robe that was upon him, and gave it to David, and his garments, even to his sword, and to his bow, and to his girdle."

As with Patroclus and Achilles, the exchanging of garments confirms a binding-together of souls. Division, a paranoid alienation, underlies the opposite scene: the pathos of

Saul's armor on David, cumbersome and unwanted: "I can-not go." Not so with these garments of Jonathan. This covenant between the two young men, homosexual or not, would wound Saul the more because of his knowledge that David's voice and harp had eased his own "evil spirits from god"—that unforgivable love-bond and benefit in his own soul complicating Saul's web of jealous despair. Many years later, David the poet will compose his great lament for Saul and Jonathan, and chant the words, "I am distressed for thee, my brother Jonathan: very pleasant hast thou been unto me: thy love to me was wonderful, passing the love of women." Repeatedly, defying the king his father, Jonathan saves David's life.

But so too does Michal. When Saul sends men to David's house, to watch all night and kill him the next morning, it is Michal who finds out about the plot and warns David: "If thou save not thy life tonight," she tells him, "tomorrow thou shalt be slain." And as in a Romantic adventure story or a thriller, she helps her young husband get away. The three crisp verbs are faster than cinematography:

"So Michal let David down through a window: and he went, and fled, and escaped."

Also in the adventure tradition—at the foundation of it?—is Michal's next subterfuge. Would elder sister Merab have been capable of this?

"And Michal took an image, and laid it in the bed, and put a pillow of goat's hair for his bolster, and covered it with a cloth. And Saul sent the messengers again to see David, saying, Bring him up to me in the bed, that I might slay him. And when the messengers were come in, behold, there was an image in the bed, with a pillow of goats' hair for his bolster."

It might be lucky for David that he was given this intrepid Michal who loved him, and not Merab the "first-born daughter" if such a phrase would have any meaning. Better for the shining poor boy David that Merab was given to Adriel (the Meholathite law student, it's tempting to say, but the stupid joke is the more inappropriate in light of what will happen to the sons of Adriel and Merab a generation later). Merab might have lacked the nerve of little sister Michal, who deceives Saul not only covertly but to his face, perhaps defying him with the transparency of her excuse:

"And Saul said unto Michal, Why has thou deceived me so, and sent away mine enemy, that he is escaped? And Michal answered Saul, He said unto me, Let me go; why should I kill thee?"

First his son Jonathan, whose "soul delighted in David," and then this unexpectedly devious, passionate girl, with her audaciously flimsy lie that she helped David because he threatened her life. That impudent token fib from Michal; Jonathan's clothes on David: no wonder Saul begins to behave strangely. As the next verses tell it, his messengers deliver the news that David is with the prophet Samuel, at Naioth in Ramah, with a company of prophets, all prophesying, which entails dancing ecstatically. At Naioth Saul's messengers feel the spirit of God upon them and they too dance and whirl in prophecy, as they report to the king.

Other messengers do the same—two detachments of them carried away by the aura surrounding Samuel the anointer who chose reluctant, moody Saul and then replaced him with eager, charming David: David now dancing with the fanatical priests as he fights with the soldiers.

So Saul himself goes to Naioth—a strange turn in the narrative, which does not say that the king went with any retinue or soldiers, or even armed himself. Is it fascination, maybe erotic, that sends Saul to go personally after the anointing prophet and the anointed harper? Something like that is what Saul's behavior, an unsated fury of attraction and even emulation, implies:

"Then he went also to Ramah, and came to a great well that is in Sechu: and he asked and said, Where are Samuel and David? And one said, Behold, they be at Naioth in Ramah." It is in keeping with Saul's thwarted and persistent character or destiny that after reports from three sets of messengers he must go to some place and inquire and then be directed to a second place. Although he is king! As though he were blundering on unfamiliar roads, cursing the swept-away messengers and the fanatical Samuel and the mesmerized Jonathan who gave David his garments and protected him from Saul's schemes, and maybe now above all the second daughter Michal: who was supposed to be a passive lure or counter, and had not only warned her husband and eased him down out of their bedroom window, and created the effigy of him for their bed, but had lied impudently about it to the king her father.

"And he went thither to Naioth in Ramah: and the Spirit

of God was upon him also, and he went on and prophesied, until he came to Naioth in Ramah. And he stripped off his clothes also, and prophesied before Samuel in like manner, and lay down naked all that day and all that night. Wherefore they say, Is Saul also among the prophets?"

"Is Saul also among the prophets?" A taunt or saying with its point blunted a little by the centuries, though the general idea is clear enough—that for this big-framed, determined, melancholy ruler and warrior the naked ecstasy is somehow inappropriate, even comical. The nakedness echoes the trading of garments between Saul and David, then Jonathan and David. And the ecstatic, stripped celebration of the Spirit of God, the abandoned male dance, will recur years later at the scene of unmitigated anger between David and Michal.

So with King Saul pathologically enraged against him David spends his years as a kind of pirate, as a rebel leader, and eventually as chieftain over his loyal troops as a turncoat follower of the Philistine king Achish. "And every one who was in distress, and every one who was in debt, and everyone who was discontented gathered to him. And he became captain over them."

In the course of things David the privateer general or Robin Hood acquires maybe a couple of dozen official concubines and wives, possibly more. Years later, when he has become king of Israel as well as Judah, the prophet Nathan will remind him that when he succeeded Saul he inherited the wives of Saul. And Michal is not the only strong personality among these women, though she may be most profoundly David's wife, emotionally the one. She is first, but the first example we get of those later wives is also an impressive woman.

In this period when David and his band of men roam the land as partisans or principled bandits, they run afoul of a man named Nabal, who inhospitably refuses their request for food—though Nabal's own young shepherds testify that David's fighters have protected them and their flocks. From Nabal's viewpoint, he may be resisting demands made by a gang of thugs. What follows Nabal's snub of David demonstrates that a wife among these people is not necessarily a passive nonentity:

"But one of the young men told Abigail, Nabal's wife, saying, Behold, David sent messengers out of the wilderness to salute our master; and he railed on them. But the men were very good unto us; and we were not hurt, neither missed we any thing, as long as we were conversant with them, when we were in the fields. They were a wall unto us both by night and day, all the while we were with them keeping the sheep."

Nabal's household is a wealthy one. Abigail quickly provides two hundred loaves and two hundred bottles of wine, and five dressed sheep, along with parched corn, raisins and two hundred fig-cakes, and has them loaded onto pack-donkeys. Then she sends the servants to go ahead of her with the plentifully laden donkeys, telling them that she will follow. "But," says the text, "She told not her husband Nabal."

On the road Abigail meets David and his armed men. He

has been thinking that Nabal's refusal to provide a little food for those who protected his shepherds must be well punished, and on this occasion David's thinking is in the vocabulary and spirit of a hardened brigand or guerilla leader: "If I leave of all that pertain to him by the morning light any that pisseth to the wall." That is, this harsh poetry means that David intends to kill every male of the household. Abigail prostrates herself on the ground at his feet and pleads with him. She uses the fact that her husband's name suggests a pun in Hebrew:

"Hear the words of your handmaid. Let not my lord regard this ill-natured fellow, Nabal, for as his name is, so is he; Nabal is his name, and folly is with him. But I your handmaid did not see the young men of my lord, whom you sent."

And more of the same, including Abigail's predictions of triumph and rule over Israel for David, a forecast proffered along with the bread, wine, raisins, sheep and fig-cakes. David in turn blesses Abigail and, in response to what might seem her coldblooded or disloyal speech regarding Nabal, he penetrates to the fact: she has prevented bloodshed: "Blessed be your discretion, and blessed be you, who have kept me this day from bloodguilt and from avenging myself with my own hand."

So David accepts the gifts of food from Abigail and she returns home to Nabal. And as for Nabal:

"And Abigail came to Nabal; and behold, he held a feast in his house, like the feast of a king; and Nabal's heart was merry within him, for he was very drunken: wherefore she told him nothing, less or more, until the morning light. But it came to pass in the morning, when the wine was gone out of Nabal, and his wife had told him these things, that his heart died within him, and he became as a stone. And it came to pass about ten days after, that the Lord smote Nabal, that he died."

Nabal who in his folly was capable of disregarding the threat of David killing him along with every single one pertaining to him that "pisseth against the wall," even the fool or jerk Nabal, when he hears the account of David's charm and good fortune from the lips of Abigail—even that same Nabal has, despite his foolishness or his security in his riches, as much insight into the truth of things as is needed to give him a stroke or a heart attack. And after Nabal dies ten days later, David "sent and communed with Abigail, to take her to him to wife."

Abigail's courage, her initiative and her blessed "discretion" in excluding Nabal from her actions amend any notion of a wife as a cipher. So that her self-abnegating response to David's marriage proposal seems ritualistic: "And she arose, and bowed herself on her face to the earth, and said, Behold, let thine handmaid be a servant to wash the feet of the servants of my lord." The next verse makes clear that David has married a woman of substance: "And Abigail hasted, and arose, and rode upon an ass, with five damsels of hers that went after her; and she went after the messengers of David, and became his wife."

So it is possible to think that the nature of marriage for David has been made clear, that it differs less from modern ideas than the biblical forms and speeches indicate. But that familiarity is undermined at once by the double shock of the last two verses in this chapter. First, immediately after the words that say the resourceful widow Abigail "became his wife" comes this terse account in the penultimate verse:

"David also took Ahinoam of Jezreel; and they were also both of them his wives."

And then the next, final verse of the chapter says:

"But Saul had given Michal his daughter, David's wife, to Phaltiel the son of Laish, which was of Gallim."

The words are so surprising one feels like reading them over again. Saul had given her to Phaltiel from Gallim! He had, he could? The story of Abigail deflects attention in a way that makes this turn in the story of Michal the more startling. Is Michal then forgotten, a closed chapter in David's long life?

No, on the contrary. Many years later, after the long war between the House of Saul and the House of David; after David has sung his great elegy for Saul and Jonathan; many wives and concubines later; after the births of David's son Amnon the firstborn, of Ahinoam of Jezreel, and Chileab the secondborn, of Abigail the widow of Nabal of Carmel, and the thirdborn, Absalom the son of Maacah the daughter of Talmai King of Geshur—these people are not all Jews— and the fourthborn Adonijah, of Haggith, and the fifthborn Shephatiah, of Abital, and the sixthborn Ithream, of Eglah; after Abner Saul's general becomes more powerful than Ishbosheth, Saul's ineffectual son and heir: after all of this, and all of these years, Abner the general representing the House of Saul sends messengers to David at Hebron, saying:

"Whose is the land? Make thy league with me, and behold, my hand shall be with thee, to bring about all Israel unto thee."

To this offer David responds with but one condition, as if he has been waiting and planning for this precise moment, not forgetting it through all those battles and marriages and sons:

"Well, I will make a league with thee: but one thing I require of thee, that is, Thou shalt not see my face, except thou first bring Michal, Saul's daughter, when thou comest to see my face."

His face, which has attracted so many, has an eerie part in this declaration. He knows his face is desired, as he knows he is in control now, but for this moment he has "one thing" in mind: Michal. Then:

"And David sent messengers to Ishbosheth, Saul's son, saying, Deliver me my wife Michal, which I espoused to me for an hundred foreskins of the Philistines. And Ishbosheth sent, and took her from her husband, even from Phaltiel the son of Laish. And her husband went with her along weeping behind her to Bahurim. Then said Abner unto him, Go, return. And he returned."

And David becomes King of Israel. And does this cruel drama with its prolonged exact memory—the specified and delivered sum of a hundred foreskins, as binding in law, not the munificent gratuitous overplus of two hundred—

demonstrate that Michal is David's one true wife? Bound to him in hurt and rage as well as in love?

Or is it not that at all, and is this rather a matter not between a man and a woman but between David and the House of Saul, the triumphant warrior in middle age recalling the insult delivered to him when he was a highminded young upstart? Is the awful pilgrimage and turning away of the weeping husband Phaltiel who must obey Abner and return the by-product of a male drama? Is Phaltiel made into something more annulled than a cuckold and more bereft than a widower for political reasons? Or is it the consequence of passion, is Michal the soulmate of David, the once-devoted pair welded together by molten anger and calamity?

King David in his triumph decides to bring the Ark of the Lord into his new city Jerusalem, in a procession, with music, sacrificial offerings and ecstatic dancing:

"And it was so, that when they that bare the ark of the Lord had gone six paces, he sacrificed oxen and fatlings. And David danced before the Lord with all his might; and David was girded with a linen ephod. So David and all the house of Israel brought up the ark of the Lord with shouting, and with the sound of the trumpet. And as the ark of the Lord came into the city of David, Michal Saul's daughter looked through a window, and saw king David leaping and dancing before the Lord; and she despised him in her heart."

The dancing recalls the days of whirling with Samuel in Ramah. The procession recalls Michal's horrible trek with her weeping husband Phaltiel, tersely commanded by Abner at the end of the journey to surrender and leave. The window recalls her helping a younger David escape from the murderous anger of her half-insane father. And the dancing and music continue.

"Then David returned to bless his household. And Michal the daughter of Saul came out to meet David, and said, How glorious was the king of Israel to day, who uncovered himself in the eyes of the handmaids of his servants, as one of the vain fellows shamelessly uncovereth himself!"

These are the unmistakable bitter tones of the unsparing, killjoy hatred that can come only from sexual love. Their quarrel is not with Saul, or even with fate, but with one another. This is the toxic attachment, the wounded desire to wound, between a man and a woman. Michal hates him not simply for inflicting that tortured march on her and her husband Phaltiel—she hates him for being himself, for being David. She hates him for what she loved in him when she was a king's daughter and he that splendid upstart. And when she looks out the window that conceivably reminds her of that other window, to see him dancing wildly, a naked or half-naked king whirling in exultation, she beholds again that same thing she loved in him, and she despises it afresh.

About his wild dancing David answers her in kind, with what can be imagined as tears of passion:

"And David said unto Michal, It was before the Lord, which chose me before thy father, and before all his house, to appoint me ruler over the people of the Lord, over Israel: therefore will I play before the Lord. And I will yet be more vile than thus, and will be base in mine own sight: and of the maidservants which thou hast spoken of, of them shall I be had in honor."

And the chapter ends:

"Therefore Michal the daughter of Saul had no child unto the day of her death."

IV

Five Golden Tumors
and Five Golden Rats

In his later years Saul—who has banned sorcerers, magicians and fortune-tellers from his kingdom—ventures in disguise to consult a witch. A great battle with the Philistines is imminent, and all sources of prophecy have failed the king.

To go in disguise is like the divided and uncomfortable soul of Saul, who hid in the baggage when it was time to be chosen as king: his long, unsought role in life which itself comes to resemble if not a disguise then an unwanted garment that has grown into his flesh, mastering him, impossible to remove as the tormenting shirt of Greek myth. Even now as his life is about to end, Saul looks fruitlessly for some refuge or advantage in concealing himself.

And the spirit that Saul asks the Witch of Endor to summon by her dark arts is the shade of Samuel, the man who grudgingly presented him with his destiny and then deprived him of its fulfillment—Samuel the giver and Saul the receiver, both from the outset reluctant and beset by misgivings. And now Saul courts the presence of that one soul among all the numberless dead most likely to spurn and torment him.

When the people first wanted a king and the Lord told Samuel to find the chosen one among the children of Israel, even at that beginning Samuel's great stinting speech to the people seems to doom Saul to frustration—consigned to rebuff before he is even anointed. Even the Lord's own instructions to the prophet, as the Late Source portrays them, are grudging: "Now therefore hearken unto their voice; howbeit ye protest solemnly unto them, and shew them the manner of the king that shall reign over them." Samuel's speech to the people, before Saul can so much as hide from that agonizing shirt of his destiny, is like a preparation for the speech Samuel will make as a spirit summoned by the Witch of Endor, at the far end of Saul's reign. Now, if the Lord is grudging, Samuel goes further toward a blighting meanness, eloquently and painstakingly. He says to the people:

"This will be the manner of the king that shall reign over you: He will take your sons, and appoint them for himself, for his chariots, and to be his horsemen; and some shall run before his chariots. And he will appoint him captains over thousands, and captains over fifties; and will set them to ear his ground, and to reap his harvest, and to make his instruments of war, and instruments of his chariots. And he will take your daughters to be confectionaries, and to be cooks, and to be bakers. And he will take your fields, and your vineyards, and your oliveyards, even the best of them, and give them to his servants. And he will take the tenth of your seed, and of your vineyards, and give to his officers, and to his servants. And he will take your menservants, and your maidservants, and your goodliest young men, and your asses, and put them to his work. He will take the tenth of your sheep: and ye shall be his servants. And ye shall cry out in that day because of your king which ye shall have chosen you; and the Lord will not hear you in that day."

It is like Saul that he must obediently accept the role described to his future subjects in this sour manner by the very man who anoints him, as it is like Saul to consult the Witch of Endor in disguise, with only a few companions: as his promised destiny failed him, prophecy has failed him. Saul the man of comfortless opposites, denounced before he is installed, willful because unwilling, bans the magic arts and needs them—as he proscribes and wants David. And the performance that is opposite to going in disguise would be David's naked whirling, the exposed performative spirit that makes both Saul's son and his daughter fall in love with the dancer: the musician-poet who was first loved by Saul himself, with that first love repeated by Saul's flesh and blood, and also by the Philistine king who makes David his bodyguard and trusted lieutenant, and also by the people, who were warned against kings before they had a king, and who sing, "Saul has slain his thousands, and David his ten thousands."

The odd, profane episode when the Witch of Endor summons the spirit of Samuel back from the dead can be seen as Saul's effort to find something like art: a third force beyond the two overwhelming principles that appear to rule his world: violence and God's will. Every practical difficulty, every hunger of the spirit, seems to be subordinate to those two realities. Only David, who can pick up the harp and sing, who can fit words together in a way that drives away the "evil spirit from God" that afflicts Saul: only David seems to have a personal power beside or additional to God's will and human violence—both of which, with an unfairness that drives Saul crazy, also and repeatedly favor David.

Magic might seem to the thwarted, melancholy king like a compromise or an alternative: relatively intimate and small-scale, personal—again like the songs of David—compared to the uncontrollable divine possession and ritual public rant of prophecy. Like poetry, magic engages immediate needs by departing from usual modes.

What is the difference between magic and religion? A quick simplifying answer might be that your religion is my magic. But another is that as religion is to strategy, magic is to tactics. Religion manifests itself in overarching practice, as regular as insurance bills; magic is more like an immediate, desperate or giddy jaunt to Las Vegas—a ploy, whereas religion is an approach. Or does religion generate an infinite contract of all-inclusive and unconcluded sentences, while magic has the specific, sweated, even monomaniacal focus of a lyric poem? Magic compared to religion has a pragmatic, literal symbolism. When it works and when it fails, magic speaks the plainest language of symbols.

In the realm of David and of Saul who banned it, magic is no amusement for children: not a mere proto-technology or

set of tricks anticipating our grand modern devices for fly-
ing through the air and seeing across the ocean and casting
our voices over thousands of miles, as in the *Arabian Nights*.
Yet magic is more technological and available than the hand
of God or the word of his prophets; in that, it resembles the
force of arms. The symbolism of magic tends toward a kind
of crude, insistent imagism. And sometimes the Philistines
use it.

For example, a generation before Saul's crowning as the
first King of Israel, during the last of the decades when the
people of the tribes of Israel are still led by themselves and
by the prophets—in the time while governing is still
divided between the Bedouin-like hierarchies of the family
and the priestly exercises of the altar—the Philistines capture the holy ark itself.

They carry the ark into the house of the fertility god
Dagon and place it near the image of Dagon and leave it
there overnight. The uncanny transpires:

"And when the people of Ashdod rose early the next day,
behold, Dagon had fallen face downward on the ground
before the ark of the Lord."

After a second night, the citizens of Ashdod wake to a
second manifestation: the idol has not only fallen; its hands
and head have been smashed off and left on the threshold
of the temple. The threshold possibly is a symbol of dangerous transitions—as taking the ark has been, and as return-
ing it will prove to be. And the breaking of Dagon is itself
merely a symbol or entryway to the real calamity:

"The hand of the Lord was heavy upon the people of Ashdod, and he terrified and afflicted them with tumors, both Ashdod and its territory. And when the men of Ashdod saw how things were, they said, The ark of the God of Israel must not remain with us; for his hand is heavy upon us and upon Dagon our god."

This epidemic is believed to be the Bubonic Plague, the horrible infection that afflicts victims with buboes or tumors. The elders of Ashdod send the ark to the city of Gath:

"And it was so, that, after they had carried it about, the hand of the Lord was against the city." And it caused "a very great panic, and he afflicted the men of the city, both young and old, so that tumors broke out upon them. So they sent the ark of God to Ekron. But when the ark of God came to Ekron, the people of Ekron cried out, They have brought around to us the ark of the God of Israel to slay us and our people. They sent therefore and gathered together all the lords of the Philistines and said, Send away the ark of the God of Israel, and let it return to its own place, that it may not slay us and our people. For there was a deathly panic throughout the whole city. The hand of God was very heavy there; the men who did not die were stricken with tumors, and the cry of the city went up to heaven."

So after death and panic spread through the city the Philistines send for priests and diviners, their best experts in magic, to advise them how the ark can be returned. The magicians (priests not of Yahweh but of gods like the mutilated Dagon) counsel that the ark must be returned with a "guilt offering" or "trespass offering": the second, more legalistic and civil-sounding English translation reminding us that the religious notion of "offering" has a secular aspect. An offering can be a settlement in the sense of a payoff, as well as a gift.

Then the Philistine lords ask their magicians for specific instructions: precisely what settlement should they offer to that murderous Hebrew deity? These Philistine elders and magicians discuss Yahweh the God of Israel with considerable familiarity, as though they had dealt with Him or at least something that resembled Him, before. The solution they specify expresses that familiarity. The bizarre, explicit and in a sense practical symbolism of what they recommend embodies not piety but magic:

"Then said they, What shall be the trespass offering which we shall return to him? They answered, Five golden tumors and five golden rats, according to the numbers of the lords of the Philistines: for one plague was on you all, and on your lords."

The magicians and wise men seem percipient not only regarding the ways of the God of Israel—they are learned enough to cite Pharaoh as a bad example!—but also of the connection between rats and the Bubonic Plague. (Though most translations say "mice," the New King James Version and some others choose "rats.")

And so, as the magicians advise, the holy object is returned on a driverless cart along with the five golden rats or mice and the five golden tumors. The driverless cart is to be pulled by two milk cows, and so those kine plod, lowing as they go, with the Philistine lords walking after them, straight down the road to Beth Shemesh, the nearest Hebrew town. At Beth Shemesh the weird, solemn procession halts when the cows stop next to a large stone in the middle of a wheat field. There at the stone the rejoicing inhabitants of Beth Shemesh break up the cart for firewood and kill the milk cows for a sacrifice. Atop the great stone they display the five golden tumors and the five golden rats, symbolic of the five afflicted Philistine cities and their lords.

The propitiatory magic of the Philistines works.

Here what might be called the efficacious, civil magic of the settlement, the golden images of rats and tumors, the milk cows—all of that merely human magic between warring sides—gives way to the more terrible, direct work of the Lord. For the rejoicing people of Beth Shemesh make a terrible mistake: in their celebration they look into the ark of the Lord, and for this he strikes out at them:

"And he slew some of the men of Beth Shemesh, because they looked into the ark of the Lord; he slew seventy men of them, and the people mourned because the Lord had made a great slaughter among the people."

The careful human magic of the enemy, with its almost childishly explicit symbols, has successfully placated the Lord. The careless, celebrating eyes of the Israelites looking directly at the holy object itself calls down great slaughter among them. What fears and desires, what view of things, underlie such a story?

A logic respectful of darkness, frugal of superiority and fortune. A logic as eerily literal in its approach to symbolism as the magic of golden tumors and golden rats. A mingled fatalism and practicality. A brisk, practical sense that in the face of God's power one goes about the businesses of life, magical or quotidian, with that all-mighty Hand hovering always over one's head. And a respect for literal-minded symbols, like the representations of the five golden tumors and five golden rats.

Saul too turns to magic, when he inquires of the Lord and gets no answer by dreams nor by prophets nor by the Urim and Thummim, the sacred objects in their little box, used like dice or the I Ching. So he asks his servants to find a woman who is a medium or "hath a familiar spirit":

"So Saul disguised himself and put on other raiment, and he went, and two men with him; and they came to the woman by night. And he said, I pray thee, divine unto me by the familiar spirit, and bring me him up, whom I shall name unto thee. And the woman said unto him, Behold, thou knowest what Saul hath done, how he hath cut off those that have familiar spirits, and the wizards, out of the land: wherefore then layest thou a snare for my life to cause me to die? And Saul sware to her by the Lord: As the Lord liveth, there shall no punishment happen to thee for this thing. Then said the woman, Whom shall I bring up unto thee? And he said, Bring me up Samuel."

When Odysseus goes to the underworld, the shade of great Achilles, hungry for the blood of life, tells him that any living peasant in the humblest cottage is happier than all the shadowy spirits of the dead. The condemned souls who address Dante, even from the darkest parts of Hell, often ask him explicitly to bring their stories to the world of light, above. In those narratives, the shades are supplicant, the living enviable, full of the rich energies of being as symbolized by the trough of blood or by Dante's weight, that displaces pebbles or lowers Charon's barge in the water as Virgil's barely substantial presence cannot. For Saul, trying to suppress his identity—and failing—the figure from the pit of Sheol seems more substantial and vital than the living man who summons him.

"When the woman saw Samuel, she cried with a loud voice: and the woman spake to Saul, saying, Why hast thou deceived me? for thou art Saul. And the king said unto her, Be not afraid: for what sawest thou?"

Like the wizards of the Philistines, the Witch of Endor understands magic, with no apparent religious attitude or standing.

"And the woman said to Saul, I see a god coming up out of the earth. He said to her, What is his appearance? And she said, An old man is coming up; and he is wrapped in a robe. And Saul knew it was Samuel, and he bowed with his face to the ground, and did obeisance. Then Samuel said to Saul, Why have you disturbed me by bringing me up? Saul answered, I am in great distress; for the Philistines are warring against me, and God has turned away from me and answers me no more, either by prophets or by dreams; therefore I have summoned you to tell me what I shall do. And Samuel said, Why then do you ask me, since the Lord has turned from you and become your enemy? The Lord has done to you as he spoke by me; for the Lord has torn the kingdom out of your hand, and given it to your neighbor, David."

"Why then do you ask me?" The magic is technically successful, since the Witch of Endor does succeed in summoning the spirit of Samuel from the pit of death, but that accomplishment reenforces the judgment of God, capricious from an objective standpoint, that Saul will be thwarted. Saul's malfeasance in either of the two tellings was petty: beginning the rituals one day without the authority of the cranky Samuel, who was late in arriving; or, in the second account, not killing quite all of the Amalekites and their livestock. That is what the revenant, sourpuss soul of Samuel tells the king. That, and also that David will thrive. The summoning of Samuel is a symbol of Saul's futility, the tall discredited king a creature of useless nerve and muscle, paralyzed by the sting of the prophet.

In the days of Saul's first glory, there was another strikingly literal symbol, involving not magic or divine will but violence. That first siege, when Saul cut up the yoke of oxen and had the parts carried by messengers around the country, to raise his army, was the doing of Nahash the Ammonite against the town of Jabesh-Gilead:

"And all the men of Jabesh said to Nahash, Make a covenant with us, and we will serve you. And Nahash the Ammonite answered them, On this condition will I make a covenant with you, that I may thrust out all your right eyes, and lay it for a reproach upon all Israel." (In the Revised Standard, "and thus put disgrace upon all Israel.")

The mere pragmatic body of conquest is insufficient, as any humiliating verbal formula of surrender would be insufficient. Nahash wants a symbol. Drastic marks and signs are required, the spirit intertwined with the body—and mutilating the body, if need be. The same eye in every case because uniformity emphasizes the disgrace, and the right eye because the dexter side is favored and therefore the more disgraceful peace offering.

Life registers its triumph over other life as a corporeal fact, a deprivation of the flesh made visible, with an explicit purpose: symbolic, and identifiably of the spirit precisely because it is functionless and gratuitous. The fearsome contract of servitude goes beyond the practical, to the spiritual. Nahash the Ammonite's proposal resembles the action of the Syracusans, who after their surprising victory over the Athenians branded their captives on the face with the image of a horse, meaning reduction of the enemy to a domestic animal. The pope's representative on his mission to correct the Cathar heretics did not stop at one eye, but blinded the lot of them completely—except for one left with his vision intact to lead the others in a procession, as a spectacle meant to fortify the Catholic faithful.

That I may put out all your right eyes and bring reproach on all Israel. Nahash wants to be clear with them: their proposed humiliation is not incidental but essential. It is part of his foreign policy. Moreover, Nahash understands that complying with his requirement would entail a certain cost or difficulty: he gives the elders of the city a week for consultations. It can be said without irony that in certain ways he is a reasonable man. His proposal has a terse and literal-minded rationality akin to the five golden tumors and five golden rats. If he is to forego exterminating his enemy, he wants an assurance whereby the symbolic and the actual reinforce one another. The leaders of Jabesh-Gilead might even in some sense have considered his specificity reassuring, a mark of civilization or at least reliability.

Nor can Nahash be called definitively more cruel or violent than the prophet Samuel, who calls upon King Saul to avenge what Amalek did generations before: "Now go and smite Amalek, and utterly destroy all that they have, and spare them not; but slay both man and woman, infant and suckling, ox and sheep, camel and ass." Here for the Hebrew prophet too the craving goes beyond practical notions of justice or strategy, and the conquest must be a spiritual matter. The horrendous scale of his command to the king is itself a symbol, representing his spiritual outrage: extravagant violence embodying the prophet's extreme righteousness as five objects might embody the distress of five cities.

So in response to the demand of Nahash for the eyes, Saul cuts up the oxen and sends the bloody parts around to the oxen-owners of his kingdom as an earnest of his recruiting methods, and the great army gathers and they rout the Philistines, slaying them all morning in such numbers that no two remain together (but not slaying Nahash, who survives to reappear as an ally of David). And Saul forbears, and disobeys Samuel's instructions regarding the Amalekites, the prophet's explicit command to "smite Amalek" and to kill every man, woman, child, nursing infant and domestic animal.

So says the prophet Samuel, because that singular or collective "Amalek" (the Amalekites) molested Israel (the patriarch and progenitor Jacob's name, as well as that of his nation) when he came up from Egypt—"Amalek" as though an individual were to be slaughtered, because of something that happened many generations ago: historical thinking as doggedly literal as magic with its symbolic embodiments.

And when Saul puts all of the Amalekite people to the edge of the sword, but forbears and takes their king, Agag, alive, and when Saul moreover allows the people to take unblemished animals as spoils for sacrifice, he is cursed forever by the Lord and Samuel. "What is the meaning of this bleating of sheep and lowing of oxen that I hear?" demands the prophet of King Saul. Then Samuel learns that Saul has spared the life of Agag the king:

"Then said Samuel, Bring ye hither to me Agag the king of the Amalekites. And Agag came unto him delicately. And Agag said, Surely the bitterness of death is past. And Samuel said, As thy sword hath made women childless, so shall thy mother be childless among women. And Samuel hewed Agag in pieces before the Lord in Gilgal."

Does the Hebrew word *ma'adanot* (מעדנות), rendered here in the King James translation as "delicately," mean *trembling* or *mincingly* or *cheerfully* or possibly *hobbled by fetters?* "Delicately" artfully welcomes all of these senses, as well as the word's associations with some dainty thing to eat, a delicacy. And this scene of a literal and symbolic cutting apart marks also the last that Samuel and Saul will see of one another in life (though not, by magical art, in death). As the next and closing passage of the chapter says:

"Then Samuel went to Ramah; and Saul went up to his

house to Gibeah of Saul. And Samuel came no more to see Saul until the day of his death: nevertheless Samuel mourned for Saul: and the Lord repented that he had made Saul king over Israel."

And now when Samuel comes up from the pit of Sheol and withholds from Saul not only forgiveness but any communication except for a renewed cursing, Saul—all but immobilized by the toxins of a dead prophet—knows that his thread is run. The ghost says to him:

"The Lord hath rent the kingdom out of thine hand, and given it to thy neighbour, even to David: Because thou obeyedst not the voice of the Lord, nor executedst his fierce wrath upon Amalek, therefore hath the Lord done this thing unto thee this day. Moreover the Lord will also deliver Israel with thee into the hand of the Philistines: and to morrow shalt thou and thy sons be with me: the Lord also shall deliver the host of Israel into the hand of the Philistines."

And Saul falls to the earth, terrified. A bear felled by a hornet. The Witch of Endor, the spirit-medium who has risked her life by defying his ban on magic at his request, has to persuade him, mercifully, before he will so much as take food. (Do her powers and her mercy represent a cloaked intervention of that forbidden Astarte, female goddess of love and sustenance? She would be a disguised deity sought by a disguised supplicant.)

Among the mass of the Philistine army marching to battle against Saul and his sons the next day is King Achish with his men—including his bodyguard and trusted commander David. How does this come to be? How can David and Saul be about to meet in combat, long after the encounter when David shows Saul his innocence? When David displays to Saul the evidence that he had the king in his power, but spared him—the spear and water-bottle from next to the bed where Saul slept, or the scrap of cloth David cuts from Saul's garment unnoticed, as if in the privy—Saul seems to forgive David utterly:

"Then said Saul, I have sinned: return, my son David: for I will no more do thee harm, because my soul was precious in thine eyes this day: behold, I have played the fool, and have erred exceedingly."

So Saul begs David's forgiveness, and blesses him, and indeed predicts great things for David. And David responds to Saul's words of renewed peace and blessings in the next scene; his thoughts about what Saul has just said—"I have erred exceedingly"—may be surprising:

"And David said in his heart, I shall now perish one day by the hand of Saul: there is nothing better for me than that I should speedily escape into the land of the Philistines; and Saul shall despair of me, to seek me any more in any coast of Israel: so shall I escape out of his hand. And David arose, and he passed over with the six hundred men that were with him unto Achish, the son of Maoch, King of Gath. And David dwelt with Achish at Gath, he and his men, every man with his household, even David with his two wives, Ahinoam the Jezreelitess, and Abigail the Carmelitess, Nabal's wife. And it was told Saul that David was fled to Gath: and he sought no more again for him."

David's shrewd skepticism resembles that of Odysseus when he is finally back to Ithaca and his patron Athena, in the guise of a youth, asks the hero who he is, and Odysseus invents an elaborate and circumstantial lie: the synopsis of an improvised novel, where any other man would be eager to proclaim himself home, and identify himself. "That," says Athena in effect about the untrusting and inventive hero, "is what I like about you." But unlike Odysseus, David is not home. He is in Gath, the country of Goliath, which gives another dimension to his adaptive, flagrant and ready shape-shifting, so different from the furtive and thwarted disguise of Saul.

The biblical account itself is shape-shifting. The first time David flees to the territory of Achish, King of Gath—or the first time the story is told in 1 Samuel—the servants of Achish warn the king against letting this visitor live:

"And the servants of Achish said unto him, Is not this David the king of the land? did they not sing one to another of him in dances, saying, Saul hath slain his thousands, and David his ten thousands?"

David lays up these words in his heart, and is "sore afraid of Achish the King of Gath." The course he decides to follow represents not the hand of the Lord nor force of arms nor magic, but David's own imagination:

"And he changed his behaviour before them, and feigned himself mad in their hands, and scrabbled on the doors of the gate, and let his spittle fall down upon his beard. Then said Achish unto his servants, Lo, ye see the man is mad: wherefore then have ye brought him to me? Have I need of mad men, that ye have brought this fellow to play the mad man in my presence? shall this fellow come into my house?"

The subterfuge of drooling and scrabbling works. David gets away from the court of Achish, and deposits his parents in safety with another foreigner, the King of Moab—his ancestor Ruth's country—and so David begins his period as a raider or privateer, leading a band of young men. Call him a warlord, or a guerilla.

But then in time David still in refuge from Saul becomes the vassal of Achish, calls himself the loyal servant of Achish. And when the Philistine hosts are gathering against the Kingdom of Israel, preparing to crush Saul, David and his troops march out with them.

Is David a traitor? Or if he is lying, and deceiving his lord Achish with false vows, does he have a plan? Perhaps to betray Achish in mid-battle? It is part of David's recurring good fortune that we do not know. In the story, with its two ambiguous tellings that jumble the sequence of narration with the sequence of events, one of the firm anchor-points is the action of the Philistine lords: they tell their colleague Achish that they do not trust David and his men as they go into battle. "What are these Hebrews doing here?" they say to Achish. And Achish responds to his fellow Philistine commanders:

"Is not this David, the servant of Saul, king of Israel, who has been with me now for days and years, and since he deserted to me I have found no fault in him to this day."

But Achish's Philistine comrades are angry with him; and they tell him,

"Send the man back, that he may return to the place to which you have assigned him; he shall not go down with us to battle, lest in the battle he become an adversary to us."

So Achish says to David, "As the Lord lives, you have been honest, and to me it seems right that you should march out and in with me in the campaign; for I have found nothing wrong in you from the day of your coming to me to this day. Nevertheless the lords do not approve of you. So go back now; and go peaceably, that you may not displease the lords of the Philistines."

We might not expect Achish to swear "as the Lord lives." We certainly would not expect David to resist, protesting his eagerness to enter the battle. David has been keeping from Achish's knowledge certain raids against the Philistines that David has made, concealing these violent excursions by the simple strategy of killing absolutely everyone in the places he attacks. Yet he says to Achish:

"But what have I done? What have you found in your servant from the day I entered your service until now, that I may not go and fight against the enemies of my lord the king?"

Achish answers David:

"I know that you are as blameless in my sight as an angel of God; nevertheless the commanders of the Philistines have said, 'He shall not go up with us to the battle.' Now then rise early in the morning with the servants of your lord who came with you; and start early in the morning, and depart as soon as you have light."

And that is how David has the good fortune not to fight against the Israelite army of Saul, and not against his beloved friend Jonathan and Saul's other sons Abinadab and Malchishua. "So David and his men rose up early to depart in the morning, to return into the land of the Philistines. And the Philistines went up to Jezreel."

And so at Mount Gelboa the Philistine army engages

the army of Israel on the day after Saul consults by magic the unyielding spirit of the dead prophet Samuel. And the Philistines kill Jonathan and Abinadab and Malchishua, the sons of Saul. But Saul, still big and athletic, fights on:

"And the battle went sore against Saul, and the archers hit him; and he was sore wounded of the archers. Then said Saul unto his armourbearer, Draw thy sword, and thrust me through therewith; lest these uncircumcised come and thrust me through, and abuse me. But his armourbearer would not; for he was sore afraid. Therefore Saul took a sword, and fell upon it. And when his armourbearer saw that Saul was dead, he fell likewise upon his sword, and died with him. So Saul died, and his three sons, and his armourbearer, and all his men, that same day together."

The Philistines, when they come "to strip the slain," find Saul's body and cut off his head, and strip off his armor and put it in the temple of Astarte. They fasten the headless body to the city wall of Beth-Shan. And the inhabitants of Jabesh-Gilead, the city rescued by Saul in his first great action as king, when Nahash threatened to gouge out their right eyes, hear about what the Philistines had done to Saul. And the men of Jabesh-Gilead go out one night and reclaim the body of Saul and the bodies of his sons from the wall of Beth-Shan, and bring the bodies back to Jabesh, and burn them there. "And they took their bones, and buried them under a tree at Jabesh, and fasted seven days."

When he hears of the defeat and death of Saul, David tears his clothes, and he fasts, and so too do David's men. And David composes and sings his elegy for Saul his king and Jonathan his friend:

The Life of David

The beauty of Israel is slain upon thy high places:
How are the mighty fallen! Tell it not
In Gath, publish it not in the streets of Askelon;
Lest the daughters of the Philistines rejoice,
Lest the daughters of the uncircumcised triumph.

Ye mountains of Gilboa, let there be
No dew, neither let there be rain, upon you,
Nor fields of offerings: for there the shield of the
     mighty
Is vilely cast away, the shield of Saul,
As though he had not been anointed with oil.

From the blood of the slain, from the fat of the
     mighty,
The bow of Jonathan turned not back,
And the sword of Saul returned not empty.
Saul and Jonathan were lovely and pleasant in their
     lives,
And in their death they were not divided:
They were swifter than eagles, they were stronger
     than lions.

Ye daughters of Israel, weep over Saul,
Who clothed you in scarlet, with other delights,
Who put on ornaments of gold upon your apparel.

How are the mighty fallen in the midst of the battle!
O Jonathan, thou wast slain in thine high places.

I am distressed for thee, my brother Jonathan:
Very pleasant hast thou been unto me:
Thy love to me was wonderful, passing the love of
    women.

How are the mighty fallen, and the weapons of war
    perished!

Who is the man—or, for that matter, if he is a figment
then what is the figment?—who writes such a poem and who
repeatedly kills all the inhabitants of a place to keep his raid
secret? Who is the creature who pleads with Achish to go
into battle against Saul and Jonathan and then laments for
Saul and Jonathan?

The enigma is heightened and epitomized by an incident
when David is faced with his own equivalent of the Bubonic
Plague and broken Dagon that confronted the Philistines,
when they made the golden rats and tumors—or his equivalent of the crisis that confronted Saul when he sought the
Witch of Endor.

His infant child is sick, and David prays and fasts and
sleeps outside on the bare earth. And the elders of his house
go to where David is, and encourage him to get up from the
bare earth; but he refuses, and keeps on fasting and praying
and prostrating himself in the dirt.

And after seven days of this fasting and praying and lying
on the dirt, the child dies, and the servants of David are
afraid to tell him:

"[F]or they said, Behold, while the child was yet alive, we

spake unto him, and he would not hearken unto our voice: how will he then vex himself, if we tell him that the child is dead? But when David saw that his servants whispered, David perceived that the child was dead: therefore David said unto his servants, Is the child dead? And they said, He is dead."

Then, here is what David does:

"David arose from the earth, and washed, and anointed himself, and changed his apparel, and came into the house of the Lord, and worshipped: then he came to his own house; and when he required, they set bread before him, and he did eat."

David's followers are mystified by their many-minded, clear-sighted master's behavior.

"What thing is this?" they say.

David's answer indicates an unfathomable command of himself, recognizing both the need for magic or piety and the boundaries of that need. He recognizes the nature of the world, including his own mortality:

"And he said, While the child was yet alive, I fasted and wept: for I said, Who can tell whether God will be gracious to me, that the child may live? But now he is dead, wherefore should I fast? can I bring him back again? I shall go to him, but he shall not return to me."

The praying, the fasting, the falling to the earth, are not dissimulated for show or for concealed motive, not a performance like his drooling onto his beard and babbling when he pretends to be crazy in the court of Achish. But the genuine praying, like the feigned madness, communicates itself to those around David with utter conviction—and like the madness the praying is directed toward a calculated end. The direct symbolism of the rats and tumors, the classic and ineffectual conjuring of Samuel by the Witch of Endor, have a childlike simplicity by comparison with David's performances, his power of simultaneous conviction and detachment.

When the fasting or the dribbling spittle onto his beard or the marching with Achish are done with, when the immortal lamentation has been composed and chanted, he proceeds to the next thing with a double-jointed certainty, nearly sincerity, that is a mystical step beyond mere egotism. Unlike the golden tumors or the precondition of gouged right eyes, David's gestures of affliction subsume their unflaunted paradoxes—purposeful grief, cunning madness—with additional levels of perspective and reservation, where *is* and *is not* occupy the same space. David attains the simultaneous engagement and calculation of art.

After the battle at Mount Gelboa, and after David's singing of his lament for Jonathan and Saul, David was crowned King of Judah. And the long war began between David in Judah and opposing him the surviving house of Saul, in the Kingdom of Israel to the north, led by the general Abner who had escorted David carrying the head of Goliath; Israel was headed by the titular heir Ishbosheth (his true name "Ish-ba'al," which scribes feared to write because it suggested idolatry), son of King Saul.

"When they told David, It was the men of Jabesh-Gilead who buried Saul, David sent messengers to the men of

Jabesh-Gilead, and said to them, May you be blessed by the Lord, because you showed this loyalty to Saul your lord, and buried him! Now may the Lord show steadfast love and faithfulness to you! And I will do good to you because you have done this thing. Now therefore let your hands be strong, and be valiant, for Saul your lord is dead, and the house of Judah has anointed me king over them."

So did David the new King of Judah, no longer a maker of raids but a ruler, address the men of the city that King Saul of Israel had rescued from the terrible proposition of the gouging-out of right eyes. And Abner the general took control of the Kingdom of Israel and the house of Saul.

"But David waxed stronger and stronger, and the house of Saul waxed weaker and weaker."

V

Smoke from His Nostrils, Devouring Fire from His Mouth

The Arab poets, who call him *Dā'ūd*, *Dāwūd* or *Dahwoud* (and call his son *Suleiman*), credit David with the invention of chain mail. A wild anachronism, but that is the man: intricate links like jeweler's mesh, the achieved lightness and suppleness that almost conceal its purpose, protection in a lethal business. A defense limber for a good offense. Military equipment that joins a convoluted sleek beauty to the implication of violent force.

Force is paramount, even in the revelations of divine will. David's lament for Saul and Jonathan would be no masterpiece, despite its excellences of reason, mystery, clarity and grace, if it lacked this essential quality. Like chain mail a poem too is a limber fabric of links, balancing flexibility with strength. The same might be said of any speech that reaches the status of action. David's eloquence can be both lyrical and political, with the force of art, or of public speech, or both.

At the level of epic action, speech and swordstroke can

equally, even simultaneously, reveal character in warfare. In epic combat, the impulsive, stained currents of emotion dig their irrevocable channels of deed and word: sudden bodily facts that the survivors for generations can neither revoke nor forget. In that realm of athletic maiming and killing, even generosity and attachment define themselves by the grim arbitrament of force. Destiny is played out on the epic field of heroes, where violence exerts its awful clarity, in the story of Abner and Joab.

Saul's general, Abner son of Ner, has moved on by the logic of a career, a worldly process doubtless as powerful as his personal ambition and possibly more inexorable. Abner has progressed to the role of kingmaker from the day when he escorted the boy David to the king's tent after that unexpected triumph.

Now Abner has made Saul's forty-year-old son, Ishbosheth, king of the northern tribes and all Israel. When Saul, cursing the stifling and itchy cloak of an ineffectual disguise, visits the Witch of Endor to learn his doom, there is no mention of Ishbosheth. We are free to imagine him pursuing the pleasures of a middle-aged and minor Saudi prince, or as the equivalent of some gentleman-farmer, maybe a harmless and even respected ophthalmologist or stockbroker whose royal blood enhances the prestige of his firm or hospital. Ishbosheth is not there to fight and fall in the terrible defeat on Mount Gelboa with his brothers Jonathan, Abinadab and Malchishua and their father. Nor is Ishbosheth mentioned when the men of Jabesh-Gilead, faithful to their debt, retrieve by night the mutilated and dishonored bodies of Ishbosheth's flesh and blood from the city walls of Beth-Shan.

So when Abner, in a gesture as primitive and unmistakable as Freud's notion of the Primal Horde, "goes in" to the concubine Rizpah who belonged to Saul, the grizzled general of course knows the rules: with all due respect to Rizpah and to sexual pleasure, Abner must mean deliberately to put the peaceable forty-year-old Ishbosheth, the rightful inheritor of Saul's concubines, in his place:

"And Ishbosheth said to Abner, Wherefore hast thou gone in unto my father's concubine?"

"Then was Abner very wroth for the words of Ishbosheth, and said, Am I a dog's head, which against Judah do show kindness this day unto the house of Saul thy father, to his brethren, and to his friends, and have not delivered thee into the hand of David, that thou chargest me to day with a fault concerning this woman?"

Abner's bullying sexual and verbal action is as lucid as when a male baboon displays his contemptuous buttocks, or pounds his dominant chest, in order to cow some rival baboon. The explicit threat that Abner adds is almost a superfluous afterthought:

"God do so to Abner, and more also, if I do not accomplish for David what the Lord has sworn to him—to transfer the kingdom from the house of Saul, and set up the throne of David over Israel and over Judah, from Dan to Beersheba."

Let no modern reader who lives more by reading and writing or buying and selling—protected as we are more by the systems and agents of government than by our own physical courage—scorn Ishbosheth's response:

"And Ishbosheth could not answer Abner another word, because he feared him."

Such is the man Abner son of Ner. He means to deal with David, even likely yield to David, from a position of power.

Abner is leading a troop of men under the nominal King Ishbosheth of Israel, when they encounter a troop who serves King David of Judah, under the command of Joab son of Zeruiah. The encounter between the two groups of young men seems at first like a courtly tournament; then like a bloody symmetrical ballet, a symbolic fantasy from the *Arabian Nights* or a dream-vision of King Arthur; finally, it resembles a scene from Homer or from an Asian action movie.

Joab and Abner lead their two opposing groups of young warriors, one from Judah and one from Israel, who meet at the pool of Gibeon:

"And they sat down, the one on one side of the pool and the other on the other side of the pool. And Abner said to Joab, Let the young men now arise and compete before us. And Joab said, Let them arise."

This sounds like some boyish competition by rule, a bruising sports event recapitulating, on a symmetrical playing field within artificial rules, the otherwise rough and governless physical challenge of competing males: like the challenge Abner threw at helpless Ishbosheth the mild. In his modern translation, Robert Alter annotates his "let the lads arise and play before us" as "clearly gladiatorial or representative combat." Instead of "play," Everett Fox devises the hyphenated "do-a-war-dance," and the New King James substitutes "compete."

However we understand the verb, it begins:

"Then they arose and passed over by number, twelve for Benjamin and Ishbosheth the son of Saul, and twelve of the servants of David."

"By number"—! The telling suggests military drill but also something like a soccer match, or a football quarterback calling signals. The next verse with its unreal symmetry maintains that idea with a nightmare calm:

"And each caught his opponent by the head, and thrust his sword in his opponent's side; so they fell down together. Therefore that place was called Helkath-hazzurim [the Field of Flints, or Sharp Swords], which is at Gibeon."

The naturalistic explanation would be that this is a tournament or fencing match gone wrong. Or some bizarrely coldblooded display devised by the two commanders? And then the narrator pulls back to place-names and geography. In any case the impossibly symmetrical choreography of this mutual slaughter makes it resemble the preliminary dumb-show that mimes the action of an Elizabethan drama. And when that main drama ensues, after this preliminary death-gavotte, the action is no longer in the dreamy if gory imagining of Malory or Scheherazade, certainly not two teams of twelve, but in the harsh accurate daylight of Homer. There is a fierce battle between the survivors on both sides. The crucial action, dragging its merciless net of foreboded doom to follow, is between Abner and Joab's brother, Asahel the fast runner:

"And there were three sons of Zeruiah there, Joab, and Abishai, and Asahel: and Asahel was as light of foot as a wild roe."

In the boyishly reckless and suicidal spirit of that death game at the pool—but here in a real mortal fight—Asahel is eager to test his prowess and display it. Abner, the older man, thinks differently:

"And Asahel pursued after Abner; and in going he turned not to the right hand nor to the left from following Abner. Then Abner looked behind him, and said, Art thou Asahel? And he answered, I am."

Abner looks behind him to question the young man over his shoulder, without stopping. The exchange between the two running warriors is like the *Iliad* and so is the action:

"And Abner said to him, Turn thee aside to thy right hand or to thy left, and lay thee hold on one of the young men, and take thee his armour. But Asahel would not turn aside from following of him."

Simone Weil's essay about the *Iliad* calls it the Poem of Force. In this Homeric passage of 2 Samuel, the fast-afoot young Asahel pursuing his elder Abner is like a negative or obverse portrait of forceful young David. The dialogue spoken while running at full speed emphasizes the literal force of the pursuit, as well as the urgent moral force at stake. The repetitions are hypnotic like a chant, but also cinematic:

"So Abner said again to Asahel, Turn thee aside from following me: wherefore should I smite thee to the ground? how then should I hold up my face to Joab thy brother?"

These people know one another better than is easily

achieved in the modern world. Part of what Abner knows is that violence itself is pursuing both him and Asahel as they run panting and shouting: violence with force beyond any killing that happens between them, violence borne by the proliferating and outrageous traditions of blood into the future. The young man, unlike Ishbosheth—could it be that Asahel imagines himself challenging his elders and so emulating the better-calculating David?—will not swerve or yield:

"Howbeit he refused to turn aside: wherefore Abner with the hinder end of the spear smote him under the fifth rib, that the spear came out behind him; and he fell down there, and died in the same place: and it came to pass, that as many as came to the place where Asahel fell down and died stood still."

We readers too stand still. The encounter has its logic— "howbeit" or "however" Asahel refuses to turn aside, so "wherefore" or "therefore" Abner suddenly stops and braces and lets Asahel run into the spear-hilt that pierces him, the more experienced man executing his fatal maneuver like an expert lacrosse player, or a forward pulling up for a jump shot. The hinder end of the older man's spear, not the point, driven into the youth by his own forward energy. The athletic logic as much as the terrible realism distinguishes this killing utterly from that stylized bloodspilling of the twenty-four young men embracing and mutually stabbing. The momentum of youth this time is not symbolic but actual.

So begins the blood feud between the two generals, Abner son of Ner and Joab son of Zeruiah. (Zeruiah was David's sister or half-sister: here again the matrilinear notion clings mysteriously around David the descendant of Ruth: as David's tribe the Ephrathites is the only one named for a female ancestor, David's kin Joab and Asahel are designated by the name of their mother.)

Some time after the killing at the pool, Abner nominally representing the titular king Ishbosheth comes to David's capital of Hebron with twenty men, for truce talks. Abner, speaking as political strongman, offers David the Kingdom of Israel to go with David's Kingdom of Judah. David responds with his demand for delivery of his wife Michal, for whom he paid the one hundred Philistine foreskins. And Abner agrees and goes in peace. But just after Abner departs on his journey back to Israel, Joab returns from a raid.

When Joab arrives at David's court in Hebron and learns that Abner has left in peace, the general remonstrates with the king:

"What hast thou done? behold, Abner came unto thee; why is it that thou hast sent him away, and he is quite gone? Thou knowest Abner the son of Ner, that he came to deceive thee, and to know thy going out and thy coming in, and to know all that thou doest."

Joab accuses Abner of deceit and spying. He does not mention to his king and uncle David that Abner is the one who drove the spear hilt-first through the belly of Joab's young brother Asahel, but David certainly must be aware of it. The narrative does not report any response by David to Joab's words against Abner. It does explicitly, maybe carefully, exonerate David in what happens next:

"And when Joab was come out from David, he sent messengers after Abner, which brought him again from the well of Sirah: but David knew it not."

The words "but David knew it not" seem almost a denial, implying an accusation. Then, again comes the abrupt overthrow of a life, reported with utter finality:

"And when Abner was returned to Hebron, Joab took him aside in the gate to speak with him quietly, and smote him there under the fifth rib, that he died, for the blood of Asahel his brother."

The killing of Abner on one plane resembles a business formality: the closing of a mortgage or contract that was agreed upon, signed and notarized at the pool of Gibeon, at the moment the skilled warrior Abner stopped and braced his spear and like a Kurosawa samurai let the fleet-footed Asahel impale himself full-tilt with his own headlong velocity, so that the blunt end penetrated through his stomach and out his back.

But on another plane, for King David, that transaction—blood-simple in the precise and ordinary code of tribal meanings—raises problems of statecraft. For David, this is no playing field of young bucks bent on their gorgeous, foolhardy ballet of mutual destruction; nor is it the mafia soldier's brutish equation of revenge for the killing of Joab's brother and David's own nephew. It is political. David must now unite the kingdoms of Judah and Israel, and he must somehow find a convincingly decent royal terrain where he can stand before his subjects, between the blood of the general Abner and Abner's house on one side—and on the other side his own powerful general Joab.

So the next verse resembles a public announcement or

policy statement by David himself. A policy statement couched as a curse:

"Afterward, when David heard of it, he said, I and my kingdom are guiltless before the Lord forever of the blood of Abner the son of Ner. Let it rest on the head of Joab and on all his father's house; and let there not fail to be in the house of Joab one who has a discharge or is a leper, who holds a spindle, or falls by the sword, or who lacks bread."

To hold a spindle apparently means to be effeminate—the entire malediction like Abner's bullying of Ishbosheth recalls the attitudes of the Primal Horde. David the leader also compels Joab—whose family he has just cursed—to participate in a ritual that we can imagine is both politically calculated and heartfelt, on David's part: heartfelt perhaps even if David may well have known that Joab would surely call Abner back to Hebron and take him aside and kill him by rule of the vendetta.

"And David said to Joab, and to all the people that were with him, Rend your clothes, and gird you with sackcloth, and mourn before Abner. And King David himself followed the bier. And they buried Abner in Hebron: and the king lifted up his voice, and wept at the grave of Abner; and all the people wept."

Thus David distinguishes himself from the ordinary man, weak like us, Ishbosheth; and also from the hotheaded Asahel; and even from the shrewd general Abner who could devise no way to avoid the blade of the vendetta. Thus too, David separates himself from Joab without losing Joab as his servant and follower. The king has conducted himself like the most successful politicians. And to make his nature the more clear, and his position in the affair of Abner's death more forceful to the people, David does more: as even the best politician could not be expected to do, he writes another poem. "And the king sang a lament over Abner":

> Died Abner as a fool dieth?
> Thy hands were not bound,
> Nor thy feet put into fetters:
> As a man falleth before wicked men,
> So fellest thou.

Where the lament for Saul and Jonathan is like a fountain, this poem is like an engraved amulet, implicit and enigmatic where the earlier dirge is full-throated. A lament for one who is betrayed rather than one who falls in battle, this poem deplores Abner's helplessness—a great soldier who became a murder victim—while letting that passive victimhood imply the worldly limits or personal limitations that brought great Abner to his death, that too much resembles the death of "a fool." (Some translations say "a base man.")

And the narration tells us that the king's poem and his fasting for Abner were a public success, as well:

"And all the people took notice of it, and it pleased them: as whatsoever the king did pleased all the people. For all the people and all Israel understood that day that it was not of the king to slay Abner the son of Ner. And the king said unto his servants, Know ye not that there is a prince and a great man fallen this day in Israel?"

And what about Ishbosheth, the middle-aged ruler, that

unwarlike and quite possibly reluctant heir to the throne of an also reluctant but warlike and mighty father? Now that Abner the strongman is dead, and now that David has seen Michal his wife walking back to him, and now that David is ready to assume the throne of united Israel and Judah, what happens to Ishbosheth?

When he hears that Abner has died in Hebron, Saul's son loses heart, "his hands were feeble," and all Israel is troubled. Among King Ishbosheth's retainers and captains of troops are two brothers, Baanah and Rechab, sons of Rimmon the Beerothite. These two military men go to the house of Ishbosheth in the heat of the day, when he is (characteristically) taking his noonday rest:

"And the sons of Rimmon the Beerothite, Rechab and Baanah, went, and came about the heat of the day to the house of Ishbosheth, who lay on a bed at noon. And they came thither into the midst of the house, as though they would have fetched wheat; and they smote him under the fifth rib: and Rechab and Baanah his brother escaped. For when they came into the house, he lay on his bed in his bedchamber, and they smote him, and slew him, and beheaded him, and took his head, and gat them away through the plain all night. And they brought the head of Ishbosheth unto David to Hebron, and said to the king, Behold the head of Ishbosheth the son of Saul thine enemy, which sought thy life; and the Lord hath avenged my lord the king this day upon Saul, and upon his seed."

Possibly the death of Ishbosheth—caught napping in a melancholy literal version of the English phrase that sneaks unwelcome into the mind—is not meant to remind us of the fool's death in David's lament for Abner. Certainly here is yet another mode of killing: the victim not killed in battle then mutilated like Saul and Jonathan; not in the stylized, Aztec-frieze manner of the twenty-four youths at the Pool of the Blades at Gibeon; not in the Homeric or cinematic combat of Asahel the swift, impaled on the blunt shaft—but in a thuggish, brisk murder by the traitorous toughs Rechab and Baanah.

When those killers bring the head of Ishbosheth to David, he does not hesitate. He reminds them what he did when a man came to him claiming to be the one who killed Saul:

"When one told me, saying, Behold, Saul is dead, thinking to have brought good tidings, I took hold of him, and slew him in Ziklag, who thought that I would have given him a reward for his tidings: How much more, when wicked men have slain a righteous person in his own house upon his bed? shall I not therefore now require his blood of your hand, and take you away from the earth?"

The head of Goliath, the head of Saul, the head of Ishbosheth. These trophies each have their meaning. David's orders regarding Rechab and Baanah maintain the language of mutilation:

"And David commanded his young men, and they slew them, and cut off their hands and their feet, and hanged them up over the pool in Hebron. But they took the head of Ishbosheth, and buried it in the sepulchre of Abner in Hebron."

And so Ishbosheth, killed while taking his midday nap, is

buried in the sepulchre of Abner, the man who went in unto Ishbosheth's father's concubine, and who conducted David with the head of Goliath into the tent of Saul.

The terrible clarity of violence finds expression in Psalm 18 (repeated in 2 Samuel), the great poem of shattering and conflagration that David composes to his God. It includes these lines:

> The sorrows of hell compassed me about;
> The snares of death prevented me;
> In my distress I called upon the Lord, and cried to
>   my God:
> And he did hear my voice out of his temple, and my
>   cry did enter into his ears.
> Then the earth shook and trembled; the foundations
>   of heaven
> Moved and shook, because he was wroth. .
>
> There went up a smoke out of his nostrils,
> And fire out of his mouth devoured:
> Coals were kindled by it.
> He bowed the heavens also, and came down;
> And darkness was under his feet.
> And he rode upon a cherub, and did fly:
> And he was seen upon the wings of the wind.
> And he made darkness pavilions round about him,
> Dark waters, and thick clouds of the skies.

Such imaginative terrors and such skillful deployment are worthy of the inventor of chain mail. David's poetic vision of a force not to be resisted recognizes the world of storm-

cloud that by his mortal intelligence and courage and eloquence and good luck—all unsurpassed on earth—David
masters for a time. The vision also implies that human mastery is provisional, frail and temporary, compared to the
mastery that issues from on High.

It seems likely that one of those brutal and miscalculat-
ing brothers Rechab and Baanah, whichever was the smarter
one of the two, would say in David's imagination or actually,
something like: *But confess the truth of your heart, O you King,
and allow that you were not sorry to see that head of Ishbosheth.* And
David, to that imagined or possibly actual challenge, would
respond in his own mind: *With this speech you show that it were
better to have cut off your tongue also, for behold it is as ill in purpose as the brain and as the hands and the feet that you have made forfeit this day.* And David might imagine or even hear Rechab or
Baanah persisting with an outrage not lessened but aug-
mented by guilt—the guilt seeming to the murderer another
reason for the king to be grateful to him and his brother for
shouldering it, and voluntarily, along with the deed itself:
*Howbeit, O King, surely you were not sorry to see borne unto you the
head of Ishbosheth of the House of Saul.* The guilt, to the thug, a
heavy object he and his brother had ported for the king, with
reward due. And David recalling Saul eased by David singing
to the harp, recalling the embrace of Jonathan who loved
David as his own soul, recalling Michal looking down and
her parting words as she helped him out the window—
David might imagine himself saying to the stupid, uncom-
prehending, stubborn and already-dead thug Rechab or
Baanah the equivalent of, *You don't know anything about it.*

When those two sons of Rimmon who murdered Ishbosheth have been executed and their headless and handless bodies are hung at Hebron, David King of Judah receives the elders and representative authorities of Israel, who come to his capital:

"Then came all the tribes of Israel to David unto Hebron, and spake, saying, Behold, we are thy bone and thy flesh. Also in time past, when Saul was king over us, thou wast he that leddest out and broughtest in Israel: and the Lord said to thee, Thou shalt feed my people Israel, and thou shalt be a captain over Israel. So all the elders of Israel came to the king to Hebron; and King David made a league with them in Hebron before the Lord: and they anointed David king over Israel. David was thirty years old when he began to reign, and he reigned forty years. In Hebron he reigned over Judah seven years and six months: and in Jerusalem he reigned thirty and three years over all Israel and Judah."

These sentences that summarize David's long and successful reign also imply that as for all mortals his life however glorious must have an ending as well as a beginning. Prophecies will tell that the reign of his house will be eternal, but David's reign on earth will not last forever. At the moment of his anointing as King of Israel, the violent story of David's rise, full of marvels, begins to yield to the equally violent and marvelous story of his reign—as a mature man, no longer as a beautiful boy.

VI

Moabitage and Mephibosheth

When David became King of Israel as well as Judah he went to war with his former allies the Philistines. He attacked the Jebusites, and though they declared that even the blind and the lame would fight to keep him off (or that the city was so fortified the blind and lame *could* keep him off), he defeated them and took the stronghold of Zion; and there he built the city he called the City of David, in its compromise location between Judah and Israel, in the land of neither, as Washington was neither Virginia nor New England: the new capital, Jerusalem.

In keeping with his new rank, he increased the number of his wives and concubines, in some cases for diplomatic and political reasons. He accepted messengers and cedar trees from Hiram, King of Tyre, along with Hiram's carpenters and masons who built David a house. King Toi of Hadadezer sent his son as envoy to King David of Israel, carrying gifts of silver, gold and bronze.

¹David fought the Philistine army in the valley of Rephaim and he smote them from Geba to Gezer. He leapt and danced

before the holy ark as it was carried into his new city of Jerusalem, defying the contempt of Michal, raging and childless in the expanded category of royal wives.

He defeated the Philistines and subdued them. He took Methegammah from them. He also defeated the Ammonites and their mercenaries the Syrians. To maintain security, he established garrisons and hamstrung the horses of captured chariots. He also conquered Moab, and he treated that country of his great-grandmother—the place where he sheltered his parents when he was fleeing from Saul—with an extreme and unexplained severity:

"And he defeated Moab, and measured them with a line, making them lie down on the ground; two lines he measured to be put to death, and one full line to be spared. And the Moabites became servants to David and brought tribute."

This incomprehensible and jaw-dropping atrocity (modern English flails for a noun) is the more bewildering because it cannot be explained by mere hatred of foreigners for being foreigners. David's military under the command of Joab included loyal mercenary armies of foreigners, the Cherethites and Pherethites. The foreign rulers King Toi and King Hiram are his friends, King Achish was his lord and protector, and this same Moab sheltered his parents and was the home of Ruth. On the other hand, Saul was directed by Samuel to exterminate absolutely all of the Amalekites, and Saul was punished for making exceptions.

"So David reigned over all Israel, and David administered justice and equity to all his people," it says, a few lines after this account of the three prostrate or supine lines of

the helpless stretched onto the ground of Moab. We can sur-
mise that "his people" means something more tribal than
national or religious—but our very terms of *tribe* or *nation* or
religion slip and buckle, as ill-fitting or problematical as
defective historical or contemporary analogies (the Pelopon-
nesian War, Rwanda, Srbrenica, death camps) for the slaughter of the Moabites: that systematic arrangement of the
victims along the ground to be measured in three equal
lengths, the seemingly mad and meticulous care to spare
one-third of them, and not as a certain number of people but
as yardage, as though *Moabite* were a kind of cloth or metal
chain.

That surviving one-third might be in effect persuaded by
the experience to think of itself not each as one Moabite,
but as so many cubits or fractions of a league of Moab, measured along the ground by the soldiers of King David. The
thinking behind the execution might resemble the prophet
Samuel's assertion of historical identity over persons and
their identities, when he takes a sword and hacks to bloody
pieces the delicate-walking King Agag who for Samuel is
Amalek.

And if the measuring and slaughtering of the Moabites
(or two-thirds of the length of them) is a legend?—possibly
some openly exaggerated boast or slander or even no more
than a figure of speech, that over credulous and scheming
centuries of transmission has taken on the color of sober
fact? Then, too, part of its effect is in that downright mini-
mal telling, as of some administrative measure all but paren-
thetical to the career and nature of David, the quick and

ever-admired killer and poet, the dancer that Saul tried and failed to pin down. Which is to say that the story retains its meaning of how dire are the nations.

The bizarre and terrible image of slaughtering people divided into three lines like so much rope recalls not just the prophet personally killing Agag but, beyond Samuel's righteous butchering, that prophet's declaration of a general divine commandment to take vengeance wholesale upon "Amalek" because of killings and violations that wind back through generations and epochs: beyond Exodus and the attack on Moses to Genesis and the twin brothers Jacob and Esau. The violent enmities are at their roots intimate, even fratricidal.

Just as Amalek the man, Esau's grandson, becomes Amalek the nation—marked for vengeance, every one of them—so too do Amalek's cousins, the people of Israel, carry a name signifying both man and nation: the new name given to Jacob, Esau's twin and his supplanter. Jacob is Amalek's great-uncle, as well as the angel-wrestler who becomes "Israel"—meaning "Struggles-with-God." That struggle of Jacob marks his becoming a patriarch, which is to say an embodied nation: "Thy name is Jacob; thy name shall not be called any more Jacob, but Israel shall be thy name: and he called his name Israel. And God said unto him, I am God almighty: be fruitful and multiply; a nation and a company of nations shall come out of thy loins."

That struggle with the angel and its outcome of the man Jacob becoming the human entity Israel endures as mysterious and dark, its obscurity falling too over the notion of "his

people" in the account of David's reign: a shadow of implication across the idea of seed or nation or company of
nations. The image of infant Jacob born holding his elder
twin Esau by the heel suggests a wrestling or competitive
struggle, on an individual level, so primal it precedes birth.
"Company of nations" indicates the redoubled plurals that a
singular identity can imply.

The younger twin born clenching the elder by his heel
squeezes into a gesture the mingled embrace and aggression
of human life, where need wrestles with competitive rage,
and the intimately familiar reverses to embody otherness.
And the one who is born wrestling with his brother later
wrestles with the angel of God.

Whatever wrestling-with-God may mean, it entails becoming a nation or a people or a company of nations: vertical in
time, a ladder destined through the ages, rather than bound
for a lifespan to move merely horizontal to the earth like
any individual creature or species. To wrestle with the angel
is to struggle beyond and before your own lifetime. What
makes me Amalek or Israel or Moab to you, and what you
might do about it, involves an intricate web of memory,
descending from one end of time and ascending to the other,
though encountered at some immediate moment. And then
in the wake of that given moment, as we brush past it, the
web is as though folded and refolded by the laddered cat's-
cradle of centuries, until little seems to remain besides that
up-and-down venous walkway of enigma, pedantic specula-
tion, entanglement and atrocity.

But repeatedly just when that recessive web seems to

envelop David, removing him from actual regard (let alone comprehension)—a being inaccessibly repellent or magnetic but either way unreadable—the story shifts, and David's character emerges as recognizable, possibly even clear and anyway immediate. These abrupt wheelings of destiny seem to hark back always to the House of Saul. When David was offered the throne of Israel, his first thought was of Michal. And now, when the new King of Israel and Judah has founded Jerusalem in Zion and solidified his reign, and established his cabinet, a different but related thought comes to him:

"And David reigned over all Israel; and David executed judgment and justice unto all his people. And Joab the son of Zeruiah was over the host; and Jehoshaphat the son of Ahilud was recorder; And Zadok the son of Ahitub, and Ahimelech the son of Abiathar, were the priests; and Seraiah was the scribe; And Benaiah the son of Jehoiada was over both the Cherethites and the Pelethites; and David's sons were chief rulers. And David said, Is there yet any that is left of the house of Saul, that I may shew him kindness for Jonathan's sake?"

The narrative by placing the question immediately after the list of officeholders presents this as though it were the new king's first thought, as Michal once was his first condition—David in triumph thinking always about the displaced family of Saul his first benefactor, and here above all of Jonathan, who contrary to his own blood ties protected David from that benefactor's prescient, mad, ambivalent but murderous enmity. As David returned to Saul's tent with the head of Goliath, his thoughts now, as if by a habit forged that day of his first military victory, return to the House of Saul.

So the courtiers bring to David a man named Ziba, who was a servant of that house, and the new king repeats his question:

"And the king said, Is there not yet any of the house of Saul, that I may show the kindness of God unto him? And Ziba said unto the king, Jonathan hath yet a son, which is lame on his feet."

This is Mephibosheth, son of Jonathan, "crippled in his feet" at the age of five when his nurse, hearing the news of Saul and Jonathan killed in battle, took flight and in her panic dropped the child, laming him. Now, speaking to Ziba, David's variation of what he says—"kindness of God," in place of the earlier "kindness for Jonathan's sake"—suggests not merely personal loyalty, but an absolute religious obligation. A conjecture might be that the question, outwardly kind, is inwardly prudent: a new ruler might have selfish political motives for knowing what heirs exist from the previous dynasty.

The lame man Mephibosheth, damaged symbolically and in his actual body by the news of the great defeat at Mount Gelboa, comes before King David and prostrates himself on the ground at the king's feet. "And David said, Mephibosheth! And he answered, Behold thy servant!"

Even though this dialogue might be useful politically to David, as a kind of caption to public display of the lame man falling on his face to do reverence, the king's behavior—

rooted as it may be in guilt or show, or policy or love for Jonathan, or all of these or none—is generous:

"And David said unto him, Fear not: for I will surely show thee kindness for Jonathan thy father's sake, and will restore thee all the land of Saul thy father; and thou shalt eat bread at my table continually."

So David instructs Ziba to till the lands of Saul for Mephibosheth, and bring in the harvest for him. And: "As for Mephibosheth, said the king, he shall eat at my table, as one of the king's sons."

But Mephibosheth was not necessarily King David's first thought upon accession, nor was Mephibosheth Saul's only surviving descendant when David became king. The episode of the famine and the Gibeonites intervenes. The blood tie; the tribal or national tie; the generosity toward Mephibosheth in the name of Jonathan who loved David; or in the name of God—all this is amplified or transformed by the story of David and the Gibeonites.

Although 2 Samuel tells the Gibeonite story some fifteen chapters after the scene between David and Mephibosheth, the matter of the Gibeonites and the three-year famine precedes that scene in time. It suggests that Jonathan's son the lame prince might well fall to the ground (like a spared or exterminated Moabite?) at the feet of King David, who was a shepherd when Jonathan the king's son loved him:

"Now there was a famine in the days of David for three years, year after year; and David sought the face of the Lord. And the Lord said, there is bloodguilt on Saul and on his house, because he put the Gibeonites to death. So the King called the Gibeonites."

The Gibeonites, in the even-then ancient history of the land, were among the Canaanites who inhabited it before the people of Jacob the God-wrestler came to it. Their case to David is against the House of Saul:

"So the king called the Gibeonites. Now the Gibeonites were not of the people of Israel, but of the remnant of the Amorites; although the people of Israel had sworn to spare them, Saul had sought to slay them in his zeal for the people of Israel and Judah. And David said to the Gibeonites, What shall I do for you? And how shall I make expiation, that you may bless the heritage of the Lord?"

The Gibeonites' answer to David's question has the terrible and splendid, oblique, nearly teasing, quality that opens negotiation and then snaps it shut with an abrupt demand—as when Saul dickers the marriage contract with David, or the Philistines confer about the ark, or Nahash names his price of the right eyes:

"It is not a matter of silver or gold between us and Saul or his house; neither is it for us to put any man to death in Israel. And he said, What do you say that I shall do for you?"

That David must repeat his question and that he rephrases it give a ritual diplomacy to this encounter. And the music of ritual and diplomacy constitutes the drumbeat prelude or accompaniment for death-dealing on a national or judicial scale:

"They said to the king, The man who consumed us and

planned to destroy us, so that we should have no place in all the territory of Israel, let seven of his sons be given to us, so that we may hang them up before the Lord at Gibeon on the mountain of the Lord."

"And the king said, I will give them."

So David takes the two sons by Saul of Rizpah, the concubine with whom Abner politically cuckolded the weak King Ishbosheth. He adds to them the five sons of Merab, that older sister Saul promised to him when he was a youth: her children by Adriel the Meholathite. And David gives all seven men, two of Saul's sons and five of Saul's grandsons, into the hands of the Gibeonites, who put them to death "in the first days of the harvest, at the beginning of barley harvest."

That is the context for David welcoming the lame son of Jonathan to eat at the king's table as one of his sons. The fiery or frozen actions of blood or nation or state, extensions of the wrestling with God or an angel, have their own scales of urgency, superhuman or inhuman as we may choose to call them. In those actions, the blood of Saul is forfeit, though it is in the veins of Jonathan's half-brothers and nephews; and a Moabite may be five or six feet of Moab. This savagery and enmity infuse the Psalms, those masterpieces of paranoia, as we should not anachronistically call them. Here is the first one traditionally designated a Psalm of David, Psalm 3:

> Lord, how are they increased that trouble me!
> Many are they that rise up against me.

Many there be which say of my soul,
There is no help for him in God,
Selah.

But thou, O Lord, are a shield for me,
My glory, and the lifter up of my head.
I cried unto the Lord with my voice,
And he heard me out of his holy hill.
Selah.

I laid me down and slept; I awaked,
For the Lord sustained me.
I will not be afraid of ten thousands of people,
That have set themselves against me round about.

Arise, O Lord; save me, O my God;
For thou hast smitten all mine enemies
Upon the cheek bone; thou hast
Broken the teeth of the ungodly.

Salvation belongeth unto the Lord;
Thy blessing is upon thy people.
Selah.

The broken teeth and cheekbones; the tens of thousands of
enemies; the terror of abandonment; the plea for a shield;
the Moabites stretched in three lines on the ground, with
two of the lines for killing; the sons of Saul hung as a famine-
price at the time of the barley harvest: these circumstances

grow from the wrestling with God, if that is the struggle that makes "Jacob" into "Israel" or "Amalek" the person into "Amalek" the nation. By comparison, the merely personal brutality that takes Bathsheba from Uriah and destroys Uriah is in a minor key.

Rizpah the concubine, after her sons have been hung to end the blood-feud and the famine, protects the bodies where they have been left as part of the expiation:

"Then Rizpah the daughter of Aiah took sackcloth, and spread it for herself on the rock, from the beginning of harvest until rain fell upon them from the heavens; and she did not allow the birds of the air to come upon them by day, or the beasts of the field by night."

Rizpah too has perhaps wrestled with God—or at least she too has an agonistic vision of blood loyalty, an identity beyond her immediate, individual circumstances as a daughter of Aiah, a concubine. When Abner went in to her and humiliated Ishbosheth the son of Saul (what word does a concubine use in place of "husband"?) Rizpah was a kind of political tool. Now her public vigil has an effect on the king, on the body politic, on the nations that inhabit the land, and on the land:

"When David was told what Rizpah the daughter of Aiah, the concubine of Saul, had done, David went and took the bones of Saul and the bones of his son Jonathan from the men of Jabesh-Gilead, who had stolen them from the public square of Beth-shan, where the Philistines had hanged them, on the day the Philistines killed Saul on Gelboa; and he brought up from there the bones of Saul and the bones of his son Jonathan; and they gathered the bones of those who were hanged. And they buried the bones of Saul and his son Jonathan in the land of Benjamin in Zela, in the tomb of Kish his father; and they did all that the king commanded. And after that God heeded supplications for the land."

VII

Thou Art the Man

In the verse immediately after the mourning of Rizpah,
right after David responds to her vigil by burying the
bones of the house of Saul—including the remains of Saul
and Jonathan as well as the seven sons and grandsons given
by David to the Gibeonites for hanging, to end a prolonged famine—the narrative takes another unexpected
turn:

"Moreover the Philistines had war yet again with Israel;
and David went down, and his servants with him, and fought
against the Philistines: and David waxed faint."

David, "faint"? That is the King James translation of the
Hebrew *vaya'aph* (וַיָּעַף). The Revised Standard says, "and
David grew weary," possibly even more startling than
"faint": because yes, even this very embodiment of male
energy might become *faint*, from some passing ailment; but
for the lethal poet-soldier who whirls and escapes and fights
and sings to become *weary*—that seems precisely unlike the
indefatigable boy and man we have known.

But David at this point in his career is, indeed, unlike the previous David. As if to enforce that point the story harks back to one of its beginnings, to Goliath the Philistine giant. The passage continues:

". . . and David waxed faint. And Ishbibenob, which was of the sons of the giant, the weight of whose spear weighed three hundred shekels of brass in weight, he being girded with a new sword, thought to have slain David."

No one can say how deliberate is that triple repetition in English (though not in Hebrew) of "weight," in its nominal and verbal forms, the very syntactical pattern ponderous, in these lines that confront the weariness of David who once trotted lightly toward outraged and immobile Goliath, the Hebrew youth's heels flickering like the sling. Now another giant, of another generation, thinks to slay the weary or woozy David. But a brother of Joab's—a man of the blood-line that David has consigned to at least one case of disease or madness or holding a spindle or lacking bread in every generation, cursed by David for killing the general Abner, cousins of David though they be—a brother of Joab and of Asahel the fast runner killed by Abner and avenged by Joab, comes to David's rescue:

"But Abishai the son of Zeruiah succoured him, and smote the Philistine, and killed him."

And the next words show that this incident of David rescued from the giant has its results, emphasizing that this is a new David, whose life has changed along with his position, different now in ways not limited to the expanded roster of wives and concubines, diplomatic and recreational:

"Then the men of David sware unto him, saying, Thou

shalt go no more out with us in battle, that thou quench not the light of Israel."

So David the King is no longer David the warrior, because he is not only the King of Israel but the Light of Israel as well: a Light not to be risked, a beacon. The reason his men give him also embodies the tact that supporters owe to the top dog. David's transformation, which is partly the transformation of anyone at all growing older and also partly the transformation of Jacob into Israel, or Amalek the man into Amalek the nation or company of nations, is part of the meaning of the first lines that tell the well-known and ugly-beyond-measure story of David and Uriah. Kings—mere kings, those who are not Lights?—go forth, but David tarries:

"And it came to pass, after the year was expired, at the time when kings go forth into battle, that David sent Joab, and his servants with him, and all Israel; and they destroyed the children of Ammon, and besieged Rabbah. But David tarried still at Jerusalem. And it came to pass in an eveningtide, that David arose from his bed, and walked upon the roof of the king's house: and from the roof he saw a woman washing herself, and the woman was very beautiful to look upon."

Present-day tourists know the walkable roofs of Jerusalem's Old City, the sun-colored stone shading the streets, the city on its distinct planes filtering and complicating the sun and conducting foot traffic on those separate levels that can be imagined governing or maybe even determining this scene of angled voyeurism. Or if that roofscape architecture does not help create the event, then something like the reverse: in the imagination of Jerusalem's builders or inhabitants, for a hundred generations, the story of Bathsheba inspiring, encouraging, that configuration of over-street and under-street that makes other cities seem to lack a dimension—however tall the skyscrapers of Chicago or Hong Kong—because at their base they have only one intimate ground level to the Old City's two or more.

So from level to level of that layered city, up from his bed and then onto his roof, to look thirstily down or across, the intricately ever-unfolding soul of David ventures and gazes, newly domesticated away from the open, sunstruck, male brute theater of battle where he first made his name. Now he has been sequestered girl-like away from combat by his own paradoxical status as the Light of Israel, separated from sieges and giants into the architectural world of beds and roofs and baths—David is inside and outside; on the roof and the ground; the Light that leads and that must be protected; in the city by political necessity and on the field of battle by political proxy through Joab his patient vicar and his Aaron, his consiglieri and cat's paw. He is the first man of the pack, and he has a new need to confirm his primacy. Compelled to hover amid these contradictions, David then decisively, as a deflected mighty soul will do, takes another course:

"And David sent and enquired after the woman. And one said, Is not this Bathsheba, the daughter of Eliam, the wife of Uriah the Hittite? And David sent messengers, and she came in unto him, and he lay with her; for she was purified from her uncleanness: and she returned unto her house."

As simple as that: the great infamous, movie-engendering,

legendary business undertaken and accomplished as quickly as that, in so few words. Actually, not as simple as the terse narrative makes it seem. And not merely because scholars read "purified from her uncleanness" as a later interpolation. The convenient symbol of the ritual bath that "purified her from her uncleanness" hadn't yet been invented, or anyway hadn't been codified, until closer to the time of the anonymous, editorial hand that the Oxford Bible says added the phrase about ritual bathing, the *mikvah*, long after the original genius had narrated this story of the bath—later to be restored to its erotic and merely secular (even Gentile?) bath-liness, by the movies.

It is not that simple, moreover, because of the immemorial, perhaps most fundamental of all human complications, disclosed by the next sentence. David in his restless mood, removed from personal combat, sent for the wife of Uriah the Hittite and she came in to him and he lay with her and she returned to her house. Might that not be the end of it? But then:

"And the woman conceived, and sent and told David, and said, I am with child."

David already has many children, many sons. And not this complicating and doomed fetus, but another child of Bathsheba's, later, will become David's great inheritor Solomon: the builder of the Temple and the worshipper of the abomination or goddess Ashtoreth or Astarte and other foreign gods, the wise man and the lover of an African queen. This earlier and problematical child is the infant that becomes ill, so that David fasts for it and tears his garments for it in prayer: the baby that dies, after which the king astonishes everyone by calmly ordering a meal and fresh clothes, because the case is closed. It is in the nature of kings and heroes to focus on what is at hand. Heroism is not nostalgic, nor is government. (This quality may be even more determinant in David than guilt, though the story says explicitly that the baby must die because it was begotten in its father's sin.)

But what is at hand now is the pregnancy and the attraction to this woman, or more than attraction (or less, the mere inconvenience of the pregnancy?); and David is decisive, general and hero and governor that he is. Decisive, and sneaky:

"And the woman conceived, and sent and told David, and said, I am with child. And David sent to Joab, saying, Send me Uriah the Hittite. And Joab sent Uriah to David. And when Uriah was come unto him, David demanded of him how Joab did, and how the people did, and how the war prospered."

Uriah the Hittite gets to chat with the king. We don't know if Uriah was called "the Hittite" because he actually was a Hittite, and not one of the children of Israel, or perhaps a convert, or if he bore "Hittite" merely as a nickname, with no more significance than "Swede" or "Yogi" or "Blackie." The matter is of interest partly because Uriah shows himself to be loyal, as well as a decent and courageous man. But be he Jew or Hittite or something in between, it seems likely that this little talk with David exerted at least some of that terror brought to an ordinary life when it has been pulled, faultlessly and without appeal, into the gravitational field of a great life.

And how is Joab doing, King David inquires of Uriah the Hittite, and tell me how the war is going. As though they were all peers or cronies together: the king inquires of the Hittite soldier Uriah after the royal vicar and counselor Joab, a relative cursed by David (partly for reasons of state) yet relied upon by David. This is the world that Uriah and Bathsheba have entered as a result of her bath and the king's restless rising from his nap.

David tries to make Uriah the Hittite a possible father of Bathsheba's baby. After that plan fails, he conspires with Joab to dispose of Uriah the Hittite—whose uprightness David's scheme tests, and who remains faithful to his soldier's oath of chastity though the seductively genial king feasts him and gets him drunk. Uriah, though drunk and possibly overwhelmed by David's company, declines to betray his vow. (Nor does he betray loyal solidarity with his celibate comrades, still at the battlefront.) He does not sleep with Bathsheba.

Contrary to the notion of David passionately in love with Bathsheba, so caught up in his passion that he does evil, the king's interview with Uriah, urging him to have another drink, suggests that David wants an alibi more than he wants Bathsheba: if Uriah violates his soldierly vow of celibacy in time of battle, if he sleeps with his wife Bathsheba as the king practically urges him to do, then David will be relieved of responsibility for the pregnancy. This is not Paolo swept up in the hurricane of his sinful love for Francesca of Rimini; David satisfies his desire and then calculates ways to avoid the unlooked-for consequence.

Uriah the Hittite keeps his vow, and that steadfastness dooms him. Uriah passes (or from another perspective fails) the test of David's plot—to seduce the man into sleeping with his own wife. And now, after Uriah returns to the war, David sends a message to Joab whose family—as punishment for a betrayal—will for generations be leprous or murdered or starving and so forth:

"And it came to pass in the morning that David wrote a letter to Joab, and sent it by the hand of Uriah. And he wrote in the letter, saying, Set ye Uriah in the forefront of the hottest battle, and retire ye from him, that he may be smitten, and die."

So Joab follows the clear, explicit directions written by the poet-king, and Uriah falls in battle, shot by archers from the walls of the besieged city: Uriah and his comrades sent into a military position that Joab and David would well know—and possibly Uriah himself and the others in the detachment also knew, even as they obeyed—was disastrous. The killing of Uriah is apparently motivated less by desire to have Bathsheba for a wife than by something like the avoidance of an ugly paternity suit.

Sending that evil letter in Uriah's own trusting or anyway obedient hand is almost too much: David not merely treacherous and ignoble, but behaving like the villain in a melodrama, an adventure-story schemer made to present the reader with a badness so consistent, so needlessly exaggerated and spelled out, that it defies ordinary prudence or common sense to pile on the nastiness. The treachery plays on Uriah's courage and his loyal obedience to duty, but why must it play on his innocence as well? Why send the message ordering this oblique murder by Uriah himself?

The effect is partly to underscore the blameless role or nature of Uriah; and maybe more, in view of the considerations that remove the Light of Israel from actual combat, in which he has thrived since childhood, to emphasize the monstrous requirements and hypertrophied passions of the king, or of kingship itself. And the frustrations or self-doubts of the king, too? A psychological understanding might assign David inward, unaware reasons for shaping his own role to be as gratuitously ugly as possible: maybe to punish himself for being away from the battle, as he punishes Uriah for being in the battle.

In a more anthropological way, giving the fatal message to Uriah for delivery is part of David's social place: to take the desirable women and impregnate them; to command the males; to demonstrate his right both to curse Joab (thus holding up the vengeance principle regarding Abner, as he does for the Gibeonites by turning over Saul's sons and grandsons) and demand Joab's loyalty (for the good of Israel); to give Uriah the Hittite his literal and figurative marching orders. In short, David is the King.

Or is David suffering from the agony that comes to the universally loved, to the beautiful boy who becomes a man? Is he nostalgic for his days as the attractive underdog who fights giants and surpasses elders—so nostalgic that he creates a giant of his own neediness and frustration, allowing himself abominable behavior because he cannot stop feeling like the underdog? Is it too elaborate that sent away from war again, now in his ascendancy, as in youth he was sent away by his elder brothers, he sets out to create a Goliath or Saul out of his own doings? Does the loss of his old underdog grace make him rationalize himself as entitled to behavior that for him is somehow defiant in the old, outlaw spirit, as well as atrocious in the new, royal status?

And what about Bathsheba, who obeys the summons and lies with the king and returns to her house and sends him word that she is pregnant? She is another woman, like Michal and Rizpah, who at first seems passive and hapless, to emerge in the end as a forcefully effective will, like Abigail. When David is very old, she will be authoritative. Bathsheba's first, present vulnerability moved the sixteenth-century Englishman George Peele to write one of the most haunting, gorgeous short lyrics of a period full of haunting, gorgeous short lyrics. The poem dramatizes her plight in the movement of the verse—by means of pauses:

BETHSABE'S SONG

Hot sun, cool fire, tempered with sweet air,
Black shade, fair nurse, shadow my white hair;
Shine, sun; burn, fire; breathe, air, and ease me;
Black shade, fair nurse, shroud me and please me.
Shadow, my sweet nurse, keep me from burning,
Make not my glad cause cause of mourning.
    Let not my beauty's fire
    Inflame unstaid desire,

> Nor pierce any bright eye
> That wandereth lightly.

The syncopated line "Make not my glad cause cause of mourning" is Peele's attempt to understand Bathsheba's apparent integrity: she obeys the king her lover, she mourns her husband, she accepts her fate with David. The graceful predicate stutter of syntax and rhythm on "cause cause," the word's energy backward and forward, is like Bathsheba's helpless need to honor her past life and her new life. Peele's spelling of her name suggests that he may have had a smattering of Hebrew, enough to know that "Bathsheba" has nothing to do with English "bath," a macaronic coincidence, but rather emphasizes her status as a woman, a daughter: "Bat-Sheba," the daughter of Sheba.

So after Joab sends Uriah into "the hottest part of the battle," as David's letter has instructed; after the words "Uriah the Hittite died also"; after Joab has carefully and cautiously conveyed that news to David; and after David has responded to the messenger with some cool words about the fortunes of war, urging his general Joab on to defeat the enemy—Bathsheba must respond. Like all those around David, including his enemies (and those who do not know if they are his enemies or his friends), she recognizes in him the quality that beyond reason or justice makes him loved. Like Uriah, she performs her duties according to law, custom and her situation:

"And when the wife of Uriah heard that Uriah her husband was dead, she mourned for her husband. And when the mourning was past, David sent and fetched her to his house, and she became his wife, and bare him a son. But the thing David had done displeased the Lord. And the Lord sent Nathan unto David."

The abrupt appearance of the prophet Nathan gives him authority, and a different moral stature than the more arbitrary-seeming and elected Samuel, who as a priest's helper heard the Lord calling him in the night. It is hard not to dislike Samuel, apprenticed to the priest Eli (whom he eclipses) as a little boy, precociously official, who sees his parents only once a year. On each of those annual visits, Samuel's mother brings him "a little robe."

Nathan simply appears and speaks, which makes him imaginable as less clerical, more appealing. Samuel seems to hector Saul, even to compete with him, dislikes the idea of a king, has tried to appoint his own no-good sons as his successors. Nathan appears concerned simply to speak truth to David. Certainly, he has the wit and rhetorical prowess to deal with a poet-king:

"And the Lord sent Nathan to David. He came to him, and said to him, There were two men in a certain city, the one rich and the other poor. The rich man had very many flocks and herds; but the poor man had nothing but one little ewe lamb, which he had bought. And he brought it up, and it grew up with him and with his children; it was used to eat of his morsel, and drink from his cup, and lie in his bosom, and it was like a daughter to him. Now there came a traveler to the rich man, and he was unwilling to take one of his own flock or herd to prepare for the wayfarer who had come to him, but he took the poor man's lamb, and prepared it for the man who had come to him."

To the bait of this parable, David rises:

"Then David's anger was greatly kindled against the man; and he said to Nathan, As the Lord lives, the man who has done this deserves to die; and he shall restore the lamb fourfold, because he did this thing, and because he had no pity."

"And Nathan said to David, Thou art the man."

And after Nathan's eloquent, detailed description of the sin, and his forecast of its consequences—the death of the infant is only the beginning—David's answer has the eloquence of brevity: "I have sinned against the Lord."

Centuries of religious and moral tradition, many thousands of words, have dealt with David's culpability and his remorse. "I have sinned against the Lord"—eloquent, brief and cogent, but in some ways unsatisfactory: what about the sin against Uriah the Hittite? Traditional understanding of the Psalms has attributed Psalm 51 to David, and to this episode of Bathsheba and Uriah:

> Have mercy upon me, O God, according to thy
>   lovingkindness: according unto the multitude of
>   thy tender mercies blot out my transgressions.
> Wash me thoroughly from mine iniquity, and cleanse
>   me from my sin.
> For I acknowledge my transgressions: and my sin is
>   ever before me.
> Against thee, thee only, have I sinned, and done this
>   evil in thy sight: that thou mightest be justified

when thou speakest, and be clear when thou judgest.

Behold, I was shapen in iniquity; and in sin did my mother conceive me.

Behold, thou desirest truth in the inward parts: and in the hidden part thou shalt make me to know wisdom.

Purge me with hyssop, and I shall be clean: wash me, and I shall be whiter than snow.

Make me to hear joy and gladness; that the bones which thou hast broken may rejoice.

Hide thy face from my sins, and blot out all mine iniquities.

Create in me a clean heart, O God; and renew a right spirit within me.

Cast me not away from thy presence; and take not thy holy spirit from me.

Restore unto me the joy of thy salvation; and uphold me with thy free spirit.

Then will I teach transgressors thy ways; and sinners shall be converted unto thee.

Deliver me from bloodguiltiness, O God, thou God of my salvation: and my tongue shall sing aloud of thy righteousness.

O Lord, open thou my lips; and my mouth shall shew forth thy praise.

For thou desirest not sacrifice; else would I give it: thou delightest not in burnt offering.

The sacrifices of God are a broken spirit: a broken and a contrite heart, O God, thou wilt not despise.

> Do good in thy good pleasure unto Zion: build thou
>   the walls of Jerusalem.
> Then shalt thou be pleased with the sacrifices of
>   righteousness, with burnt offering and whole burnt
>   offering: then shall they offer bullocks upon thine
>   altar.

God in this world, by this king, is offered not burnt meat, and not golden rats or tumors, but "a broken spirit" and "a broken and contrite heart." The ritual bullocks would be offerings reserved for some unachieved time.

If we follow the traditional view that this monumental, still-reverberating poetry that inspired Donne and Herbert is the work of David, writing in anguished contrition about the taking of Bathsheba and the death of Uriah, then the outrageous verse is the one that begins: "Against thee, thee only, have I sinned." Not against Bathsheba, or Uriah? Or against the other soldiers sent with Uriah to the hot part of the battle, under the wall where the best archers were stationed to slaughter them? Not against Joab who was told to send them there? Or even against David's own child who according to the prophet dies in infancy for David's sin? Or the negated and pre-doomed line of Uriah?

In his great nineteenth-century German translation and edition of the Psalms, Rabbi Samson Raphael Hirsch attempts to give the verse a more distinct logic. His version, in the Gertrude Hirschler English translation, inserts "therefore":

"Against Thee, and against Thee alone, have I sinned and

done that which is evil in Thy sight; therefore Thou art just in Thy speech and pure in Thy judgment."

Hirsch gives the following commentary:

These words irrefutably show that, according to the teaching of our sages, David's sin with Bathsheba and his conduct toward Uriah were violations of the spirit rather than the letter of the legal code of the land. But in the sight of God both these acts of David were grievous crimes. "Therefore," David tells the Lord, "Thou art justified in all that Thou has told me through Nathan, and in any decree that Thou wouldst wish to ordain against me. I willingly accept my punishment in advance because I am aware of my guilt."

About the logic of "therefore," Hirsch adds a parenthesis: (The word למען is used several times in the Scriptures to denote "therefore." If, however, למען should be interpreted, as it usually is, to mean "so that," then אדע and נגד in [the preceding verse] would have to be understood to denote not merely a tacit perception of one's guilt, but an explicit vocal confession to others, למען, "so that" all the world might know that the Lord is just in any punishment that He might inflict upon David. However neither the actual wording nor the facts in the case would support this latter interpretation. The criminal nature of David's acts was quite clear; the few extenuating circumstances were not nearly so obvious. Therefore we would not be wrong if in this case, too, we would interpret למען to mean "therefore."

Across Hebrew, German, English and across centuries,

the moral point meditated is whether the consequences Nathan forecasts for David will be unqualified by ambiguous covert commands, administrative murders hedged by equivocation and rationalization. Beyond the absorbing spectacle of Rabbi Hirsch's moral and philological attention, there is his point that David will endure more than human justice, on some level above persons. He has killed, therefore the infant of Bathsheba dies. He has betrayed, therefore his own house and blood rise against him. He has spoken glibly about the sword and those who fall by it, therefore the sword will never depart from his house. By the letter of the law, Uriah dies by the fortune of war.

By the letter of the law, everyone who went to war customarily wrote a bill of divorcement for his wife (enabling her to remarry if he became one of the missing), so Bathsheba was a divorcée. Some of the sages go so far as to claim that David did not sin, that he contemplated the act with Bathsheba but did not go through with it! Even more bizarre is the magnificently offensive Cabalist tradition that interprets the whole incident symbolically: as a repetition of Adam's original sin (in keeping with Psalm 51's "Behold, I was shapen in iniquity; and in sin did my mother conceive me"). In this repulsive and ingenious interpretation, Adam's name is an anagram of the initials *Adam-David-Messiah* and David repeats the First Sin in order to rectify it—by killing Uriah the Hittite, who represents the primordial serpent! So (in profound contrast with Rabbi Hirsch's למען) say certain Cabalists.

In such weird exonerations of David, inventive almost

beyond belief, sometimes transgressive of ordinary decency as well as common sense, in such insistent need for David's ultimate or transcendent righteousness, in tortuous efforts to reverse Nathan's denunciation, we can read the hungers and terrors of the Diaspora. In Babylon, and later oppressed and vilified by the European inheritors of an offshoot sect grown universal, at best tolerated and often enough tortured, these Jewish scholars need their king. They crave David as the Light of Israel, and to defend him they engage in moral twistings and outlandish inventions as distorting as the privations of Babylon, or the vicious pronouncements of Christendom itself.

For example other Talmudists, desperate to find for David some alibi or scrap of mitigation, have concocted another legend: when he had killed his kinsman Goliath, David discovered that the giant wore so many layers of complicated armor that he could not penetrate them to sever the head. Uriah the Hittite, from the Philistine camp, had the key to Goliath's armor and volunteered to trade it for an Israelite wife. So Uriah got Bathsheba dishonorably—so say those sages crazed by fasting and exile, by piety and by a surrounding majority culture that would obliterate that piety of the Jews, or failing that would obliterate Jews themselves: at best tolerating them and in Europe eventually indeed exterminating them. In the provisional shelter of the study house the scholars read the texts and commentaries obsessively, discuss them and drowse over them, and—pondering their King David, and doubtless aware of the Christian attempts to expropriate their king, their Light—they dream up these unlikely legends of exculpation.

And yet, how can they? Here is what the prophet Nathan says to David:

"And Nathan said to David, Thou art the man. Thus saith the Lord God of Israel, I anointed thee king over Israel, and I delivered thee out of the hand of Saul; and I gave thee thy master's house, and thy master's wives into thy bosom, and gave thee the house of Israel and of Judah; and if that had been too little, I would moreover have given unto thee such and such things. Wherefore hast thou despised the commandment of the Lord, to do evil in his sight? thou hast killed Uriah the Hittite with the sword, and hast taken his wife to be thy wife, and hast slain him with the sword of the children of Ammon. Now therefore the sword shall never depart from thine house; because thou hast despised me, and hast taken the wife of Uriah the Hittite to be thy wife. Thus saith the Lord, Behold, I will raise up evil against thee out of thine own house, and I will take thy wives before thine eyes, and give them unto thy neighbour, and he shall lie with thy wives in the sight of this sun. For thou didst it secretly: but I will do this thing before all Israel, and before the sun."

The youth who overcame the giant and surpassed both his humble father Jesse and the paternal figure of Saul; the son who by being the youngest son is additionally junior by the number of older brothers he will exceed—now Nathan tells him of his child, Bathsheba's infant: "because by this deed you have utterly scorned the Lord, the child that is born to you shall die." Furthermore, another son will rise against him, and will sleep with his wives, and everyone will know it. Now David who has been the quintessential son takes up the destiny, the emotional and moral vulnerabilities, of the father.

The prophet Nathan who speaks these dire, unequivocal words to the king is not older than David, or even the same age—the prophet is younger than the king, another mark of a transition for this youngest son, Saul's favorite and supplanter. The two older generals who appear at the temporal boundaries of David's career, Abner at the outset and Joab at the close, both contain in their names the syllable *ab:* "father." Abner is "Father-of-Light" and Joab (or Yoav) is "God-Is-Father." The syllable is common in Hebrew names, but it is worth noting in these dual sentinels at David's entry and departure: rivals, both of them worldly and proficient, both eventually defeated, killer and killed—those men of power bracket David's progress. In his vigil over Bathsheba's dying child we see David take only his early steps under the burden of fatherhood. He has many wives and concubines. Therefore, he is father to many children.

VIII

Sons of David

After the first infant born to David and Bathsheba dies, "David comforted Bathsheba his wife, and went in to her, and lay with her: and she bare him a son: and he called his name Solomon: and the Lord loved him."

But Solomon is far down the birth order of sons, as his mother comes rather late in the order of wives. The order of sons is explicit and precise: first, Amnon by Ahinoam the Jezreelitess; second, Chileab by Abigail the widow of Nabal the foolish Carmelite; third, Absalom by Maacah the daughter of King Talmai of Geshur; fourth, Adonijah by Haggith; fifth, Shephatiah by Abital; sixth, Ithream by Eglah.

Those are the sons born to David in his southern capital of Hebron. Later, after David became King of Israel as well as Judah, in Jerusalem, Solomon takes his rank—which is not first—in the birth order of the later, Jerusalem sons: Shammuah, Shohab, Nathan, Solomon, Ibhar, Elishua, Nepheg, Japhia, Elishama, Eliada, and Eliphelet.

Daughters are not included in these catalogs of names, but a daughter figures in the first story of the sons of David.

The story, following soon after the telling of David and Bathsheba, is also sexual and is also ugly:

"And it came to pass after this, that Absalom the son of David had a fair sister, whose name was Tamar; and Amnon the son of David loved her. And Amnon was so vexed, that he fell sick for his sister Tamar; for she was a virgin; and Amnon thought it hard for him to do anything to her."

"To do anything to her"—in the crude, even practical language the King James translators achieve a directness not merely judgmental but starkly definitive. Amnon the first in line, David's heir and the son of Ahinoam, desires to "do something to" his half-sister Tamar, the full sister of Absalom son of Maacah. And Absalom is second in line of seniority after Amnon. (Abigail's son Chileab having died, apparently; though there is a strange tradition that Chileab was so just and studious, he was allowed to enter Paradise alive.) Here is a glimpse into the ways and standards of these, what, stripling warlords or regal thugs or restless, indulged princes?—none of the above, of course, our terms and analogies all inadequate: because she is a virgin it will be difficult for him to do anything to her.

But Amnon finds a subterfuge that in its way echoes David's deviousness regarding Uriah. And as though firstborn Amnon were not already contemptible enough, he needs an advisor to help him with the subterfuge:

"But Amnon had a friend whose name was Jonadab the son of Shimeah, David's brother. Now Jonadab was a very crafty man. And he said to him, O son of the king, why are you so haggard morning after morning? Will you not tell me?

Amnon said to him, I love Tamar, my brother Absalom's sister."

So those multiple and superceded brothers, to whom father David once on a boy's errand delivered cheeses, who may have resented David's pride and his insolent heart, reappear by progeny in the form of crafty and subtle Cousin Jonadab, ready with a scheme for the son of the king. Almost lost in the primary shock of the disgusting scheme itself is the ancillary shock of David the quick one as a dupe: in this context not Hamlet or Laertes but a gulled Polonius, or some credulous father from Roman comedy:

"And Jonadab said unto him, Lay thee down on thy bed, and make thyself sick; and when thy father cometh to see thee, say unto him, I pray thee, let Tamar my sister come, and give me meat, and dress the meat in my sight, that I may see it, and eat it at her hand."

The man who has deceived the Philistines by drooling and pretending to be crazy, who once eluded Saul by easing himself out a window and leaving behind an effigy, who once skipped confidently toward hapless Goliath, and who not long ago with duplicitous geniality asked Uriah how the war was going—here takes the minor role of the malleable, unseeing duffer:

"Then David sent home to Tamar, saying, Go now to thy brother Amnon's house, and dress him meat."

The narrative that sometimes speeds through massacres in one summary phrase here becomes excruciatingly circumstantial:

"So Tamar went to her brother Amnon's house; and he was laid down. And she took flour, and kneaded it, and made cakes in his sight, and did bake the cakes. And she took out a pan, and poured them out before him; but he refused to eat. And Amnon said, Have out all men from me. And they went out every man from him. And Amnon said unto Tamar, Bring the meat into the chamber, that I may eat of thine hand. And Tamar took the cakes which she had made, and brought them into the chamber to Amnon her brother."

The cinematic deliberateness of the pace, like the repetitions "my sister," "thy brother," "her brother," the preparation of the cakes, the dismissal of the standers-by, all intensify the horror of the process. But "cinematic" indicates only the perspective of any reader as audience or spectator to this elaborated incestuous rape—and under or above the threshold of awareness any reader will feel the perspective of David, the unsuspecting father of Tamar and Amnon and Absalom (and for an extra measure of humiliation, the uncle of that crafty nephew Jonadab). Or if cinematic, then as if the deception and rape were punctuated in montage by images of David going in effect innocently—though the adverb might be forfeit to Uriah the Hittite—about his business. If Jonadab has the family cleverness, Amnon demonstrates at least for some minutes his father's actorly gift for dissimulation. Then he no longer needs to fake sickness or gentleness:

"And when she had brought them unto him to eat, he took hold of her, and said unto her, Come lie with me, my sister. And she answered him, Nay, my brother, do not force me; for no such thing ought to be done in Israel: do not thou this folly. And I, whither shall I cause my shame to go?"

Her question about her shame is far from unfamiliar

or remote. But Tamar's next words to Amnon demand a footnote:

"And as for thee, thou shalt be as one of the fools in Israel. Now therefore, I pray thee, speak unto the king; for he will not withhold me from thee."

Marriage to a half-sister was allowed in the time of David, though later forbidden. Therefore, Tamar's presumably desperate (and far from enthusiastic) "He will not withhold me from thee" directly refers to David, and so to his role here as a manipulated authority. Amnon does not spare his beautiful sister, and the narrative does not spare the reader from realism, literal or psychological:

"Howbeit he would not hearken unto her voice; but, being stronger than she, forced her, and lay with her."

Moreover: "Then Amnon hated her exceedingly; so that the hatred wherewith he hated her was greater than the love wherewith he had loved her. And Amnon said unto her, Arise, be gone."

Like the combat when Abner impales Asahel, like David's treachery toward Uriah, this encounter will have large consequences. Amnon's repulsiveness is defined with a sharper outline by Tamar's clarity. She responds to the princeling's "Arise, be gone":

"And she said unto him, There is no cause; this evil in sending me away is greater than the other that thou didst unto me. But he would not hearken unto her. Then he called his servant that ministered to him, and said, Put now this woman out from me, and bolt the door after her. And she had a garment of diverse colors upon her: for with such robes were the king's daughters that were virgins appareled. Then his servant brought her out, and bolted the door after her."

Uglier than the killing that brings the vendetta of Joab against Abner, as calculated as David's murderous betrayal of Uriah, like those events this familial rape tears the fabric of lives apart in a widening, accelerating gash. The forces are aligned and identified before they are put in motion. Absalom seems to know what has happened, and toward his sister his tone seems almost dismissive, as though the rape were merely incidental to her, and now a business of his, the dishonored second in line of succession, and not hers:

"And Tamar put ashes on her head, and rent her garment of divers colours that was on her, and laid her hand on her head, and went on crying. And Absalom her brother said unto her, Hath Amnon thy brother been with thee? But hold now thy peace, my sister; he is thy brother; regard not this thing. So Tamar remained desolate in her brother Absalom's house."

"Regard not this thing"! "Hold now thy peace"! Though Absalom tells Tamar not to regard the thing, nor to speak out, he does not mean that it is over for himself. Nor is it over for any of the other males concerned:

"But when King David heard of all these things, he was very wroth. And Absalom spake unto his brother Amnon neither good nor bad: for Absalom hated Amnon, because he had forced his sister Tamar."

And that is the last appearance of Tamar. She is accorded a legend in the same spirit of the sages who imagined that Uriah the Hittite won Bathsheba by demanding an Israelite bride from David as the price for unlocking the armor that covered the corpse of Goliath. In the volume of Talmud called Sanhedrin, it says that since Tamar was born before her mother's conversion to Judaism, her relation to Amnon is less sinful than if they had been Jewish brother and sister in the strictest sense.

The silence between Amnon and Absalom, the two senior brothers, continues in a suspended miasma of rage and culpability until two years later, when Absalom announces a sheepshearing festival, to which he invites David. When the king declines in order not to overburden his son's estate with a royal retinue, Absalom suggests that Amnon and all the king's other sons attend instead. David's questions and responses ("Why should he go with you?") suggest both apprehension and a new, ineffectual quality in dealing with the generation that comes up after Nathan's curse.

So the sons of David all attend the festival of Absalom's sheepshearing at Baalhazor, and Absalom sees to it that Amnon does not survive the gathering. This is no longer the period when King Saul hurls his own spear at David, nor is this killing personal as when Joab takes aside Abner for private conversation, and puts the blade into him. These royal sons who have servants to expel the victim after a rape also have minions to perform fratricide:

"Now Absalom had commanded his servants, saying, Mark ye now when Amnon's heart is merry with wine, and when I say unto you, Smite Amnon, then kill him, fear not: have I not commanded you? Be courageous, and be valiant."

And so it happens: Absalom gives the word and the servants kill his brother Amnon—and it remains clear that this still is the story of David. The reaction of the sons who witness the abrupt assassination in the middle of a fraternal party is perhaps surprising: they fear for their lives, and they get out, in far fewer words than are devoted to Tamar's preparation of the cakes: "Then all the king's sons arose, and every man gat him upon his mule, and fled." The sons of the beloved one, the inventor of chain mail and composer of the Psalms—the heirs of the boy who killed lions and bears and then slew the giant champion of the Philistines—flee not as a group, familial or otherwise, but as scattering eminences who suspect a massacre.

Nor is that suspicion to be dismissed as merely nervous or soft. It is plausible enough that the rumor of it comes presented to David as fact, and while the sons are still fleeing the sheepshearing, each man to his mule, their father believes the rumor:

"And it came to pass, while they were in the way, that tidings came to David, saying, Absalom hath slain all the king's sons, and there is not one of them left. Then the king arose, and lay on the earth, and all his servants stood by with their clothes rent."

What does this peculiar phantom event, a massacre that does not happen, signify? Its effect is to bring the story emphatically away not only from the desolate Tamar (trebly unconsidered now by Amnon her raper, Absalom her avenger and David her father) but away also from all these brothers and back to David—who can not only imagine such a mass fratricide, but believe it. To demonstrate how

David's increase of glory and power are shadowed by the prophet Nathan's curse, he is ministered to by that busy, clever plotter, Amnon's advisor Jonadab:

"And Jonadab, the son of Shimeah David's brother, answered and said, Let not my lord suppose that they have slain all the young men the king's sons; for Amnon only is dead: for by the command of Absalom this has been determined from the day he forced his sister Tamar. Now therefore let not my lord the king take it to heart that all the king's sons are dead; for Amnon alone is dead."

So when the sons come back in a dustcloud, each on his mule, cousin Jonadab who knows so much and divulges his role so little can claim some credit with the king:

"And Jonadab said unto the king, Behold, the king's sons come: as thy servant said, so it is."

That this cool-of-mouth, enterprising young manipulator comforts David manifests the web of suspicion, intrigue and violence foretold by the prophet as fruit of David's corruption in the matter of Bathsheba and Uriah. Now Absalom the beautiful firstborn flees the country, to Geshur where his mother's father is king. David mourns Amnon, but in an echo of how his grief was countered by his pragmatic self-mastery regarding the death of Bathsheba's first baby, David moves on: "And the soul of king David longed to go forth unto Absalom: for he was comforted concerning Amnon, seeing he was dead."

So David's heart is with the living son. But Absalom has committed a crime: he has killed King David's heir. Constrained by ambivalence or by public policy, David cannot simply embrace the exiled son he longs for—or he cannot until after some decent interval. When three years have passed, Joab devises a way to persuade (or rather allow) David to decree what his own soul longs for: Absalom's return. Possibly it is those other sons, who took each to his mule apprehending bloodshed, who now are reluctant to see the open fratricide Absalom return. The three years may seem to Joab the right interval for cooling fears and condemnations. The means Joab chooses to persuade or justify David's pardon of Absalom is a narrative—a tale similar in design to Nathan's parable of the rich man who took the poor man's lamb as David took Bathsheba. Joab sends a "wise woman" to David, and "Joab put the words in her mouth."

Joab instructs this woman to disguise herself as a mourner. She brings the king a story of her two sons, who competed in the field with no one there to part them, and one killed the other. Now, Joab instructs her to say, the family is demanding that the survivor forfeit his own life for the life he took from his brother: "and so they will quench my coal which is left, and shall not leave to my husband neither name nor remainder upon the earth."

And of course when David promises her that her son will be spared she springs the trap and begs him—in respectfully obsequious terms—to allow the return of his own banished: "as an angel of God, so is my lord the king to discern good and bad: therefore the Lord thy God will be with thee."

David is still David, though he has been played upon by the likes of Jonadab, and therefore no fool:

"Then the king answered and said unto the woman, Hide

not from me, I pray thee, the thing that I shall ask thee. And the woman said, Let my lord the king now speak. And the king said, Is not the hand of Joab with thee in all this? And the woman answered and said, As thy soul liveth, my lord the king, none can turn to the right hand or to the left from aught that my lord the king hath spoken: for thy servant Joab, he bade me, and he put all these words in the mouth of thine handmaid."

David strives to see truly through the numbing and isolating haze of deference: a drama visible as he deals with the wise woman and the more so when he detects Joab behind her masquerade. The king summons Joab. The general prostrates himself before his king, with his face to the earth. And David relents and orders Joab to go to Geshur and bring Absalom back to Israel—though the young man remains forbidden to so much as see his father: "So Absalom dwelt two full years in Jerusalem, and saw not the king's face."

Absalom's next move, his way of gaining full reinstatement, is as extravagantly willful as some legend of the frontier or the doings of mafia bullies or archaic Greek heroes. His action resembles Saul's dismembering of the oxen, both symbolic and violently literal, impressive in its recklessness. But Absalom's manner is not that of Saul, newly anointed, but that of a young aristocrat (his maternal grandfather is a foreign king, and with the death of Amnon he has become the eldest son of David).

Absalom wants Joab to intervene for him again, to secure David's recognition and acceptance, as through the wise woman he secured David's permission to return. He wants to see the king his father's face. But first Absalom must get Joab's attention—it has been two years, and after Absalom sends for Joab twice, and the general does not respond, Absalom takes another approach, as expressive of himself as the playacting of the wise woman was expressive of Joab, who chooses not to obey Absalom's second summons:

"Therefore Absalom sent for Joab, to have sent him to the king; but he would not come to him: and when he sent again the second time, he would not come. Therefore he said unto his servants, See, Joab's field is near mine, and he hath barley there; go and set it on fire. And Absalom's servants set the field on fire. Then Joab arose, and came to Absalom unto his house, and said unto him, Wherefore have thy servants set my field on fire? And Absalom answered Joab, Behold, I sent unto thee, saying, Come hither, that I may send thee to the king, to say, Wherefore am I come from Geshur? it had been good for me to have been there still: now therefore let me see the king's face; and if there be any iniquity in me, let him kill me."

If setting his ally's barley field on fire is insane, it represents insanity applied purposefully: as a threat and as a token of Absalom's terrible earnestness. Joab has gone to David that first time, to advocate Absalom's return, because "he perceived that the king's heart went out to him." Absalom's return was what David wanted anyway, and Joab devised a way to manage it. Now, Joab avoids responding to Absalom's messages, possibly because the young man's character is clear to the experienced general and courtier—and if so, then doubtless so clear that Joab is inclined to restrain

David's heart from going out too far toward Absalom, for the sake of peace and of David himself. But Absalom's gangster tactic of the burned barley field seems to leave Joab no choice. He goes to David and speaks on Absalom's behalf; and the king relenting sends for his son: "and when he had called for Absalom, he came to the king, and bowed himself on his face to the ground before the king: and the king kissed Absalom."

Years have passed since Amnon's conference with Jonadab concerning Amnon's desire for his half-sister. Absalom is himself a father: "And unto Absalom there were born three sons, and one daughter, whose name was Tamar: she was a woman of a fair countenance."

And Absalom is reinstated, recognized by the king, a presence again in the capital, the senior man among those brothers who at the killing of Amnon ran each man to his mule. And Absalom may be a little crazy, but he is more than a mere hothead. He is more calculating, as well as more ambitious, than that:

"After this Absalom got himself a chariot and horses, and fifty men to run before him. And Absalom used to rise early and stand beside the way of the gate; and when any man had a suit to come before the king for judgment, Absalom would call to him, and say, From what city are you? And when he said, Your servant is of such and such a tribe in Israel, Absalom would say to him, See, your claims are good and right; but there is no man deputed by the king to hear you. Absalom said moreover, Oh that I were judge in the land! Then every man with a suit or cause might come to me, and I would give him justice. And whenever a man came near to do obeisance to him, he would put out his hand, and take hold of him, and kiss him. Thus Absalom did to all of Israel who came to the king for judgment; so Absalom stole the hearts of the men of Israel."

IX

Would God I Had Died for Thee

David's marriage to Maacah the daughter of Talmai, king of Geshur, may have been diplomatic and political, but their offspring were attractive. Beauty in Maacah's daughter Tamar was great enough to cause a tremendous calamity—her beauty, like Bathsheba's, a "glad cause cause of mourning." And of Maacah's son Absalom the scripture says, "in all Israel there was none to be so much praised as Absalom for his beauty: from the sole of his foot even to the crown of his head there was no blemish in him."

Certain Talmudists in their ardent, bookish imaginings have declared that Absalom was a giant. In one midrash cited by Louis Ginzberg: "of such gigantic proportions that a man who was himself of extraordinary size, standing in the eyesocket of his skull, sank in down to his nose." This awestruck and outlandish fantasy conveys a scholar's pious dread at the idea of the son who defies his father the giant-killer. It also suggests an ambivalence about power itself, a minority culture's fear of monstrously large powers, maybe extending unconsciously even to David himself.

The image of the immense eye is also a symbol of unbridled greed. Like his brother Amnon, Absalom does seem a prince consumed by restless, unfillable avidity. But Absalom's greedy gaze fastens on something larger, and vaguer, than an incestuous sexual craving that burns itself out in the getting. Absalom's beauty, too, becomes a cause for mourning: because it possibly encourages him to see himself, in the immense eye of imagination, as not just supplanting David but becoming him.

In such an overgrown vision, Absalom with his expectation to be loved would be less a spoiled prince than the eager, emulative child of a man who beyond merely expecting to be loved has indeed been loved—by Jonathan and by Michal; by Philistine and by Jew: loved for something in his nature and sometimes, as perhaps by Bathsheba, in spite of his nature.

So that Absalom's flaw is less the overindulgence of privilege than his delusion that good looks and good fortune could make him the equivalent of David: the indulgence and the delusion comprising Absalom's fatal psychology. And leading, eventually, to David's grief at his son's fate. John Dryden in his *Absalom and Achitophel* writes of Absalom:

> What e'r he did was done with so much ease,
> In him alone, 'twas Natural to please;
> And *Paradise* was open'd in his face.
> With secret Joy, indulgent David view'd
> His Youthful Image in his Son renew'd.

As Dryden sees it, David shares Absalom's delusion that the son is a fresh iteration of the father. Neither David nor Absalom himself can see that there is a difference between the son's blemishless, pleasing charm and the father's quality far beyond the magnetism of charm: David's inner force of mind, even more kinetic than it is magnetic—a compound, even tormented energy that carries David to his destiny. To that force, mere attractiveness is an incidental grace note. Paradise may be opened in Absalom's face for those people he greets and chats up at the gates of court—but to be popular is not to be chosen.

The story of David is a story of flawed fathers, of unexpectedly powerful women and of defiant sons. The sons include Jonathan who resists Saul, and scoundrels who defy decency, like the sons of Eli the priest, who (unlike Eli's exemplary boy helper Samuel) embezzle sacrifices and lie with the women who serve at the entrance to the meeting-tent. Absalom's name, like "Joab" and "Abner," contains the Hebrew *ab* for "father"; in an almost excessive irony, "Absalom" means "Father-of-Peace," expressing both David's wishes and their thwarting as prophesied by Nathan.

Amplifying his physical beauty with the chariot and the fifty attendants running ahead of it, Absalom at the same time works to present himself as a generous man of the people, greeting those who come to the court for a royal audience or judgment. The grand chariot and the little chats at the gateway embody Absalom's largely successful campaign to combine the appeal of two different sorts of leader—though there is a third kind he can never become.

One type appeals by seeming born to rule: commanding by force of blood, upbringing and expectation, like Moses raised in the royal house of Egypt or like Solomon, the graceful son of a king, who will be kissed on the lips by Victory in all he undertakes, as if by royal birthright. Looking at King Lear's face, Kent reads authority there and wishes to follow it, he says; and the implication is that the regal Lear was born printed with that quality, as we are born with our chins and noses.

A second kind of leader takes authority not from that inherited hierarchical elevation written on the face or active in the blood, but from being one of us folk: expressing our nature almost by knowing us before we know ourselves, with a heightened competence that epitomizes some gift we can aspire to, but exaggerated heroically: the mighty roughneck Samson, the proficient soldier Joshua, the thriving patriarch Abraham, the faithful bruiser Beowulf. Something of the kind may be represented (or attempted?) by Absalom's offering judgment as a neighborly candidate at the gate; but also by his reckless violence that incinerates barley fields, avenges Tamar's rape, sends the terrified princes running for their mules.

Absalom, with his unblemished features and his retinue of fifty but also with his willingness to stand by the gate, flattering those who enter by talking to them, combines the two categories: he is the elegant scion of the ruling class and he is also the hypertrophied man of the folk. There is an earnest, calculated ambition to Absalom in this dual project, and he fulfills it. One can imagine him being advised in it.

We reserve our most intense feelings for a third figure, who leads neither by birthright nor as one of us, but by sheer, monstrous force of personal talent: or, to put it differently, by the love of God or the gods or fate—and that is not Absalom. *I am here leading you*, such a ruler all but says, *neither by my ancestors nor by my companions—but by myself, because the Lord has made me the most resourceful, the quickest, the best.* As David says to Michal when she denounces his dancing, he is the beloved not only of the serving girls and the soldiers and the people who chant his praises, but of God. The Lord loves him, and so do people. That is in David, like a talent: deeper than ambition and superior to calculation, with mere political usefulness a by-product: a corollary of his larger character or destiny.

But while the contest between David and his son may be a matter of character or destiny, it takes place as a matter of actual politics. Part Moabite, the former bodyguard and follower of a Philistine king, now as King of Israel protected by his loyal Cherethites and Pelethites, David unlike his predecessor Saul has had close relations with Philistines, Canaanites, all manner of non-Jewish tribes. To some of the people of Israel he might seem practically a foreigner himself. Indeed, in Talmudic discussion the question is raised whether David, as a descendant of Ruth the Moabitess, is worthy to be included in the assembly of Jews at all! The legend that David was Jesse's son by a foreign slave is used to explain why David was assigned to guard flocks, and at first not even presented to Samuel.

Absalom too is the son of a foreign woman, but he has grown up in the land of Israel. Unlike his father, he is not an outsider. Gazing at the father's origins as a nobody, that gigantic, greedy eye would begin to perceive its own head-start as a deprivation, resented. Certainly Absalom has more than once heard the story of the hundred foreskins, and the calculated magnificence of the hundred extra foreskins. It is impossible that he has not heard of the chant, *Saul has slain his thousands, and David his ten thousands.*

In any case, the young prince with his long hair, his chariot and his confiding, attentive manner succeeds in recruiting not only supporters among all the tribes of Israel; Absalom enlists his father's almost mystically wise and insightful counselor Achitophel, as well. Or the reverse: does Achitophel recruit Absalom—the subtle, ambitious counselor perceiving that a son beautiful from head to foot, quick to show his readiness for violence to Joab, might have daydreamed transformation of the chant: *David has slain his ten thousands, and Absalom* . . . ? For some four years after their official reconciliation, the son, doubtless guided by Achitophel, campaigns to gather support against the father. David's apparent failure to notice the developing rebellion could be one more frustration for Absalom: another form of exile from his father's notice.

Old tribal jealousies and unsettled accounts help the conspirators as much as David's alien qualities and Philistine entanglements. For example, it is not forgotten that David gave the Gibeonites the seven sons and grandsons of Saul to hang, as price of blood-guilt. There are other echoes of the house of Saul in Absalom's rebellion, as in every other phase of David's life. When the traitorous son Absalom wants to be proclaimed king and displace his father, he goes to Hebron, the capital of David when he ruled Judah but not

Israel. Absalom tells his followers to shout, when they hear a signal on the trumpet, "Absalom is king at Hebron!" This cry recalls David's course toward victory over Saul's house, and attempts to cast David in the role of Saul.

So the rebellion erupts, fed by historic factions, rivalries and suspicions. When the report comes from Hebron to David in Jerusalem, he returns to the tactics of his youth: he flees into the countryside with his followers. David evacuates his forces from the City of David, leaving ten concubines to watch over his house. Now once-banished Absalom can behold the spectacle of the father banished from Jerusalem by action of the son. The exodus of David's forces, the loyal supporters who accompany the king as he flees his city, demonstrates how many of David's followers have been drawn from outside the children of Israel:

"And the king went forth, and all the people after him; and they halted at the last house. And all his servants passed by him; and all the Cherethites, and all the Pelethites, and all the six hundred Gittites who had followed him from Gath, passed on before the king. Then the king said to Ittai the Gittite, Why do you also go with us? Go back, and stay with the king [meaning Absalom!]; for you are a foreigner, and also an exile from your home. You came only yesterday, and shall I today make you wander about with us, seeing I go I know not where? Go back, and take your brethren with you; and may the Lord show steadfast love and faithfulness to you."

These are Philistines and other foreigners: a "Gittite" is one from the Philistine city of Gath, as was Goliath. David's dialogue with Ittai is the model for thousands of adventure

stories where comrades choose to fight together, their loyalty transcending differences of origin, though an honorable
way out is offered. To David's offer of that honorable exit,
Ittai responds in the heroic or *comitatus* tradition (yet echo-
ing David's gentile ancestor Ruth, pledging loyalty to Jewish
Naomi, though released from any bond as David releases
Ittai):

"But Ittai answered the king, As the Lord lives, and as my
lord the king lives, wherever my lord the king shall be,
whether for death or for life, there also will your servant
be. And David said to Ittai, Go then, pass on. So Ittai the
Gittite passed on, with all his men and all the little ones who
were with him. And all the country wept aloud as all the
people passed by, and the king crossed the brook Kidron, and
all the people passed on toward the wilderness."

In this exchange, Ittai reaffirms that he sees in David the
quality he chooses to follow—the ingredient that dooms
Absalom because it is lacking in him. While Absalom strives
to emulate young David by having himself declared king
in Hebron, David without hesitation or doubt acts as he
has before by retreating into the wilderness with his band of
followers.

The priests of the Lord, too, begin to follow David into
the wilderness with the holy ark; but David tells them to
return with the ark to Jerusalem—for reasons that, characteristically, are partly noble and partly shrewd: David man-
aging things so that his pious resignation to the Lord's
judgment will also give him a valuable network of spies in
Jerusalem. He says:

"Carry the Ark of God back into the city. If I find favor in the eyes of the Lord he will bring me back and let me see both it and his habitation; but if he says, 'I have no pleasure in you,' behold, here I am, let him do to me what seems good to him. The king also said to Zadok the priest, Look, go back to the city in peace, you and Abiathar, with your two sons, Ahimaaz your son, and Jonathan the son of Abiathar. See, I will wait at the fords of the wilderness, until word comes from you to inform me. So Zadok and Abiathar carried the Ark of God back to Jerusalem; and they remained there."

David weeps as he leaves Jerusalem, climbing the ascent of the Mount of Olives, supplanted by the son his heart longed for, and needed to see again, even though Absalom killed Amnon his firstborn—moreover, even though David believed Absalom capable of killing all the king's sons. So in his compounded grief David covers his head as he weeps, and so too do his followers. One who did not know David might interpret the covered head and the weeping as evidence that the king has been unmanned. Even Absalom might think so, witnessing the moaning, hooded figure climbing the Mount of Olives. But at the summit, Hushai the Archite comes to meet the king, Hushai "with his coat rent and earth upon his head." And David may be weeping, with his head covered, but he has not lost his quickness. Having just set up the priests Zadok and Abiathar as his spies, the king now creates a double agent—he says to Hushai the Archite:

"If you go on with me, you will be a burden to me. But if you return to the city, and say to Absalom, 'I will be your servant, O king; as I have been your father's servant in time past, so now I will be your servant,' then you will defeat for me the counsel of Achitophel. Are not Zadok and Abiathar the priests with you there? So whatever you hear from the king's house, tell it to Zadok and Abiathar the priests. Behold, their two sons are with them there, Ahimaaz, Zadok's son, and Jonathan, Abiathar's son; and by them you shall send to me everything you hear. So Hushai, David's friend, came into the city, just as Absalom was entering Jerusalem."

The tumble of proper names evokes this period of conspiracy and counter-conspiracy. It also evokes David's command of the situation.

Next, the House of Saul again enters the narrative directly, in a series of encounters like Shakespearean subplots. As the displaced King David passes the summit and continues his flight into the wilderness, he meets Ziba the servant of lame Mephibosheth, the son of Saul lamed as an infant on the day of Saul's ultimate defeat at Mount Gibeon. Ziba comes with "a couple of asses saddled, and upon them two hundred loaves of bread, and an hundred bunches of raisins, and an hundred of summer fruits, and a bottle of wine." Ziba tells David, "The asses be for the king's household to ride on; and the bread and summer fruit for the young men to eat; and the wine, that such as be faint in the wilderness may drink."

A proven survivor and riser, Ziba has chosen David over Absalom. Of his master the lame son of Saul who prostrated himself on the ground at David's feet, and who ate at David's table with the sons of the king, the servant Ziba gives this report:

"And the king said, And where is thy master's son? And

Ziba said unto the king, Behold, he abideth at Jerusalem: for he said, To day shall the house of Israel restore me the kingdom of my father."

David, in another turn of his relation to Saul and Saul's children, tells Ziba that from now on all that did belong to Mephibosheth will now belong to Ziba. Next as David proceeds on his retreat from Jerusalem, a second survivor of Saul's household appears: Shimei, the son of Gera, hooting and sputtering. The scene is like something from Kurosawa, or one of the lower incidents in Homer. It is calculated to show the humiliation of David, and then his forbearance. As the king's party walk along the road, they are jeered at from the hillside opposite the road:

"And when king David came to Bahurim, behold, thence came out a man of the family of the house of Saul, whose name was Shimei, the son of Gera: he came forth, and cursed still as he came. And he cast stones at David, and at all the servants of king David: and all the people and all the mighty men were on his right hand and on his left. And thus said Shimei when he cursed, Come out, come out, thou bloody man, and thou man of Belial: the Lord hath returned upon thee all the blood of the house of Saul, in whose stead thou hast reigned; and the Lord hath delivered the kingdom into the hand of Absalom thy son: and, behold, thou art taken in thy mischief, because thou art a bloody man."

The cursing, the stones, the unseemliness of throwing both stones and curses at the king and at the "mighty men," the crazed imprecations, the zany disorder of the scene itself—all dramatize and parallel the larger reversal

of order, the father deposed by his son. Shimei would seem
to be risking his life for this opportunity to insult David and
his retinue; and indeed he is risking his life. Joab's brother
Abishai, the man who has rescued David from the giant Ishbibenob in battle—and therefore another reminder for
David that the wheel of generations is turning—speaks up:

"Then said Abishai the son of Zeruiah unto the king,
Why should this dead dog curse my lord the king? let me go
over, I pray thee, and take off his head. And the king said,
What have I to do with you, ye sons of Zeruiah? so let him
curse, because the Lord hath said unto him, Curse David.
Who shall then say, Wherefore hast thou done so? And David
said to Abishai, and to all his servants, Behold, my son,
which came forth of my bowels, seeketh my life: how much
more now may this Benjamite do it? let him alone, and let
him curse; for the Lord hath bidden him. It may be that the
Lord will look on mine affliction, and that the Lord will
requite me good for his cursing this day."

In the curving, secret logic of all narrative, in imitation of
life itself, this moment of restraint is like an assurance that
David will triumph over the rebellion. *It may be that the
Lord will look on mine affliction, and that the Lord will requite me
good for his cursing this day.* And so it will come to pass. Politically, David knows that the spectacle of the unseemly cursing will create his moment of sympathy, a longing for a
restoration of the king's dignity. Theologically, it is as if
David eagerly pays this price to the Lord, enduring the spit-
ting and stone-throwing for his sins, in order to gain the
greater goal.

And psychologically, by rising above Abishai's unreflecting urge to kill the comically ineffectual, half-crazy Shimei, David reasserts his own superiority. David's sense of drama, that instinct of poet as well as hero, seems to inform him as a strategist—as it tells us who follow the story that by touching bottom with the insults of Shimei, David will proceed to rise. David appears to know this, his grief inscrutably divided between his ordeal of the sorrow Absalom has brought him and his ordeal of the sorrow he knows he must bring to Absalom.

In that light, David's behavior toward Ziba and Mephibosheth and Shimei and Abishai—forbearing and authoritative, empathic and assured, scolding Abishai and rewarding Ziba—is the behavior of the king as an idealized father. As Absalom's burning the field is a flawed, excessive imitation of Saul butchering the oxen, his political stratagems in the end collapse into imitations of the seemingly effortless judgments of the ruddy, always confident underdog father. And David's eerily tolerant endurance of Shimei is like his apparently endless ability to forgive and spare Absalom. This incident of Shimei seals both David's coming victory over Absalom and his grief over Absalom. The actual events of whispering conspiracy and consequent battle-grunt, deception and bloodshed are the mere visible wake of this mournful but supreme assurance in David, the assurance that can afford to reprimand Abishai and let Shimei live on, jabbering and throwing dirt from above the road.

In Jerusalem, the legendary wise man Achitophel shrewdly (if obscenely) tells Absalom to treat David just as the general Abner treated Saul's weak heir: the young man should take the women David has left behind to watch over his house. And everyone should know it. The public indignity will make it clear that Absalom has overthrown his predecessor. The element that the violation is perpetrated by the son upon the household of the father will make the act all the more successful as policy. Says Achitophel:

"Go in unto thy father's concubines, which he hath left to keep the house; and all Israel shall hear that thou art abhorred of thy father: then shall the hands of all that are with thee be strong. So they spread Absalom a tent upon the top of the house; and Absalom went in unto his father's concubines in the sight of all Israel."

Achitophel, in some accounts, is the grandfather of Bathsheba. The roof, along with the sexual transgression, recalls her story, with David's abhorrent part in it. But Achitophel's insight that going in to the concubines will strengthen Absalom politically, by making the break with David more absolute and passionate, seems to have inspired Dante to assign Achitophel into one of the lowest regions of Hell: among the fomenters of schism and discord. In the *Inferno*, Dante has the beheaded shade of Bertran de Born invoke this moment in David's story:

Reaching the bridge, the trunk held the head up high
　　So we could hear his words, which were, "Look well,
　　You who come breathing to view the dead, and say

If there is punishment harder than mine in Hell.
　　Carry the word, and know me: Bertran de Born,
　　Who made the father and the son rebel

The one against the other, by the evil turn
   I did the young king, counseling him to ill.
   David and Absalom had nothing worse to learn

From the wickedness contrived by Achitophel."

The body separated from the head as the son was separated from the father—Dante cannot be said to exaggerate Achitophel's influence. The scriptural simile for Achitophel's reputation as a wise counsel is extraordinary: "Now in those days the counsel which Achitophel gave was as if one consulted the oracle of God; so was all the counsel of Achitophel esteemed, both by David and by Absalom."

This taking of the concubines is as unexpected as David's sparing of the rock-throwing Shimei: gestures in a family drama, but also moves in a contest between David and Achitophel, with Absalom's doom foretold by his role as a chess piece. Achitophel advises Absalom to let him pursue David at once, with an armed detachment, while David and his troops are weary from their retreat. In that discouraged state, David's people will abandon him. "I will strike down the king only," promises Achitophel, "and I will bring all the people back to you as a bride comes home to her husband."

But then Absalom calls for advice from Hushai the Archite—David's man, pretending to serve Absalom. In the interest of David, Hushai advises the opposite of Achitophel: that Absalom wait, and put off any pursuit of David until all of Israel is gathered behind the new king, from Dan to Beersheba. Hushai persuades Absalom with a fantasy of glorious, total conquest that appeals to the prince who likes to cut a figure in his chariot with fifty attendant runners, and who was pleased to burn down a man's field in order to get his attention. Conceivably, Absalom finds this image of victory over his father more glorious than Achitophel's proposal. Hushai:

"I counsel that all Israel be generally gathered unto thee, from Dan even to Beersheba, as the sand that is by the sea for multitude; and that thou go to battle in thine own person. So shall we come upon him in some place where he shall be found, and we will light upon him as the dew falleth on the ground: and of him and of all the men that are with him there shall not be left so much as one. Moreover, if he be gotten into a city, then shall all Israel bring ropes to that city, and we will draw it into the river, until there be not one small stone found there."

Absalom and his cohort prefer this hyperbolic, even poetic plan to the quick, surgical strike against David recommended by Achitophel—a bad decision that the narrative ascribes to the Lord's desire to bring evil upon Absalom.

So Hushai the Archite brings word of the decision to the priests Zadok and Abiathar, David's agents, and they send the information by messenger to David, who crosses the Jordan to safety with all of his people. Leaving Absalom, presumably, to gloat over the concubines—and over visions of his future triumph, with his minions pulling the very stones of some city into a river.

And Achitophel? What does the wise man do next? A tradition in midrash is that Achitophel gave instruction to many students—including the Athenian wise man Socrates. Achitophel is in other words the embodiment of intelligence and therefore not only of intelligence's limitations but the understanding of its own limitations. Possibly the idea that Achitophel taught Socrates also indicates an overdone, prodigal dispensing of wisdom: Achitophel the wise man imprudent, sharing his gift promiscuously with Greeks, as with the inconstant hothead Absalom. Now, Achitophel comprehends with a collected, despairing certainty what Absalom's decision will mean:

"And when Achitophel saw that his counsel was not followed, he saddled his ass, and arose, and gat him home to his house, to his city, and put his household in order, and hanged himself, and died, and was buried in the sepulchre of his father."

The terms *his house, his city, his household, his father* enforce from a new direction that this is an upheaval of domestic, as well as national, forces. Achitophel's suicide, like the hemlock for Socrates, acknowledges the continuity of the civic with the domestic and the personal.

As Achitophel can foresee—and as David assisted by his spies and agents can foresee—Absalom then crosses the Jordan into the land of Gilead. He has replaced Joab as head of the army with Amasa (yet another cousin related to the house of Jesse). This is Absalom's chance to revise the chant, to hear the women sing, *Absalom has killed his ten thousands.* On the other side, David is again a military leader, and for a moment he even conceives that he might again be a warrior, carrying his weapon into battle:

"And David numbered the people that were with him, and set captains of thousands, and captains of hundreds over them. And David sent forth a third part of the people under the hand of Joab, and a third part under the hand of Abishai the son of Zeruiah, Joab's brother, and a third part under the hand of Ittai the Gittite. And the king said unto the people, I will surely go forth with you myself also. But the people answered, Thou shalt not go forth: for if we flee away, they will not care for us; neither if half of us die, will they care for us: but now thou art worth ten thousand of us: therefore now it is better that thou succour us out of the city. And the king said unto them, What seemeth you best I will do. And the king stood by the gate side, and all the people came out by hundreds and by thousands."

A general but not a combatant now, David is also a father—still protective of Absalom:

"And the king commanded Joab and Abishai and Ittai, saying, Deal gently for my sake with the young man, even with Absalom. And all the people heard when the king gave all the captains charge concerning Absalom."

All the people heard, but as surely as the nation needs for the king not to risk his life in this battle, Absalom must die this day.

The forces of David demolish Absalom's army in a great rout. In the confusion, the servants of David come across Absalom, riding his mule, and in a bizarre image of helplessness and stupid, headlong disaster, his mount wedges Absalom by the head into the low-hanging branches of a tree. The usurper is suspended in a state like incomplete birth, neither on earth nor in heaven, partway-enwombed in the delivery into death, a hapless man of nowhere, puppetlike. The mule like the kingdom or like the course of life continues on without him, though he is presumably still beautiful "from the sole of his foot even to the crown of his head." Absalom is made immobile and vulnerable by his own reckless force.

Dealing with this situation, the character of Joab reveals itself, even more clearly than when he took it upon himself to kill Abner:

"And Absalom rode upon a mule, and the mule went under the thick boughs of a great oak, and his head caught hold of the oak, and he was taken up between the heaven and the earth; and the mule that was under him went away. And a certain man saw it, and told Joab, and said, Behold, I saw Absalom hanged in an oak. And Joab said unto the man that told him, And, behold, thou sawest him, and why didst thou not smite him there to the ground? and I would have given thee ten shekels of silver, and a girdle. And the man said unto Joab, Though I should receive a thousand shekels of silver in mine hand, yet would I not put forth mine hand against the king's son: for in our hearing the king charged thee and Abishai and Ittai, saying, Beware that none touch the young man Absalom. Otherwise I should have wrought falsehood against mine own life: for there is no matter hid from the king, and thou thyself wouldest have set thyself against me."

Joab listens to the "certain man," who speaks in the voice of the ordinary citizen. Joab is not the ordinary citizen:

"Joab said, I will not waste time like this with you. And he took three darts in his hand, and thrust them into the heart of Absalom, while he was still alive in the oak. And ten young men, Joab's armor-bearers, surrounded Absalom and struck him, and killed him. Then Joab blew the trumpet, and the troops came back from pursuing Israel; for Joab restrained them."

Joab demonstrates the strategic thinking of a general: his decisive restraint in battle, toward the fleeing army; and his decisive action regarding Absalom—the man Joab spoke for when Absalom was in exile from Israel, and spoke for again when he was in exile from David's face. Now, three darts to the heart.

After the news of Absalom's death comes to David, Joab shows another kind of steel in his nature, as well:

"And the king was much moved, and went up to the chamber over the gate, and wept: and as he went, thus he said, O my son Absalom, my son, my son Absalom! would God I had died for thee, O Absalom, my son, my son!"

So David's grief manifests itself. The poet who wrote great elegies for Saul and Jonathan, who reconciled himself to the deaths of Bathsheba's first baby and even of Amnon, here is neither stoical nor eloquent. Or, his eloquence is in the repetition of a name—and in what is probably hyperbole: "would God I had died for thee." After the weeping and the repetitions of the name in the chamber of the gate, David repeats it again, in his house, when his victorious army returns to the city:

"And the victory that day was turned into mourning unto

all the people: for the people heard say that day how the king was grieved for his son. And the people gat them by stealth that day into the city, as people being ashamed steal away when they flee in battle. But the king covered his face, and the king cried with a loud voice, O my son Absalom, O Absalom, my son, my son!"

In one legend, David's eightfold repetition of Absalom's name as he grieves has the effect of bringing Absalom—undeservedly by his own merits—into Paradise, or in some versions into the most elevated and privileged part of seven-fold Hell. Another legend associates the eight times David laments with the fact that eight of his sons die young, including the anonymous first baby born to Bathsheba. These narrative interpretations suggest the agony of David's perception that his own nature is at the root both of Absalom's rebellion and its doom. David the father could not protect his son from the fatal and irresistible undertaking of trying to become David.

But a king, particularly a charismatic and inspiring king, has no emotions that are merely personal—as Joab must remind David. Aware that David's mourning has made the soldiers who risked their life for him carry themselves "as people being ashamed steal away when they flee in battle," Joab becomes rather magnificent:

"And Joab came into the house to the king, and said, Thou hast shamed this day the faces of all thy servants, which this day have saved thy life, and the lives of thy sons and of thy daughters, and the lives of thy wives, and the lives of thy concubines; in that thou lovest thine enemies, and hatest thy friends. For thou hast declared this day, that thou regardest neither princes nor servants: for this day I perceive, that if Absalom had lived, and all we had died this day, then it had pleased thee well. Now therefore arise, go forth, and speak comfortably unto thy servants: for I swear by the Lord, if thou go not forth, there will not tarry one with thee this night: and that will be worse unto thee than all the evil that befell thee from thy youth until now."

This bold ranking-out calls on David's nature, and restores his attentive soul back to his kingship. Joab calls David to himself, and David responds. He unites Judah and Israel again. He holds court. Before him comes Shimei, that sputtering thrower of dust, insults and stones on the road out of Jerusalem—Shimei now abjectly begging David's forgiveness, and David magnanimously—or perhaps shrewdly, maybe even capriciously—tells the man "You shall not die," giving Shimei his royal oath to that mercy.

Before him too comes Mephibosheth the son of Saul. The lame man has not trimmed his beard nor washed himself since the king left Jerusalem. "Why did you not go with me, Mephibosheth?" asks David; and Mephibosheth answers that Ziba his servant slandered him and tricked him when he tried, despite his lameness, to ride after his benefactor David. With the confidence of disdain, and maybe even with a thought of Jonathan who loved him, or even of Michal and impressing her from a superior position, or taunting her with mercy toward her brother, David declines to judge between Ziba and Mephibosheth, though one or the other certainly is lying: "I have decided," he says, "you and Ziba shall divide the land." And Mephibosheth too is a king's son, and understands largeness: "Oh, let him take it all," he says, "since my lord the king has come safely home."

These merciful dispositions may be associated with David's cries of "Absalom, Absalom," that name meaning "Father-of-Peace." Certainly the power to dispense mercy is one aspect of David's restored authority. Another decision David makes—perhaps with reuniting the kingdom in mind; and perhaps wary of Joab's independent and murderous ways; or perhaps as a corrective to Joab's audacity in calling the king away from grief for Absalom; or maybe most of all because it is Joab's hand that drove the three darts into the heart of helpless Absalom—is to replace Joab as head of the army with Amasa.

David deals too with the additional civil war that ensues, in the aftermath of Absalom's rebellion, between the men of Israel and the men of Judah. And here David shows that while he can be merciful with Shimei and lordly with Mephibosheth, the king has not lost his ability to punish, or his power to kill. A "worthless fellow" named Sheba, the son of Bichri, a Benjamite (like Saul), blows the trumpet and raises the cry:

> We have no part in David,
> Neither have we inheritance in the son of Jesse:
> Every man to his tents, O Israel.

"Every man to his tents"—the old tribal resistance; and the men of Israel for a time actually withdraw from David and follow the lout Sheba, with the men of Judah remaining loyal to David. But David weathers that rebellion too, sending Joab to subdue the rebel when Amasa falters.

Joab deals with Amasa rather as he dealt years before with Abner, earning David's curse even before the killing of Absalom:

"And Joab's garment that he had put on was girded unto him, and upon it a girdle with a sword fastened upon his loins in the sheath thereof; and as he went forth it fell out. And Joab said to Amasa, Art thou in health, my brother? And Joab took Amasa by the beard with the right hand to kiss him. But Amasa took no heed to the sword that was in Joab's hand: so he smote him therewith in the fifth rib, and shed out his bowels to the ground, and struck him not again; and he died. So Joab and Abishai his brother pursued after Sheba the son of Bichri."

And the kingdom unites again, with the head of the worthless fellow Sheba the son of Bichri thrown over the wall from within the city where he was besieged by Joab and his brother Abishai. David succeeds. According to a tale recounted by Louis Ginzberg, when Achitophel the teacher of Socrates hung himself he left a last will, codifying three rules: "1. Refrain from doing aught against a favorite of fortune. 2. Take heed not to rise up against the royal house of David. 3. If the Feast of Shevuot falls on a sunny day, then sow wheat."

The final, absurdist yet sardonic element in the list recommends obedience to tradition, respect for the oldest precepts about good timing: a planting-time antecedent of the harvest-time figure "Ripeness is all." All three precepts—

respect for fortune, for David, and for timing—are violated by the unblemished, gigantically deluded and mourned-for Absalom, and after Absalom as if in parody by the inconsequential fool Sheba, son of Bichri.

"O my son Absalom, my son, my son Absalom! would God I had died for thee." The classical tragic hero moves from exaltation to the punishing self-knowledge of a defeat that grows from the hero's nature; David moves from exaltation to the punishing self-knowledge of his perennial and foredoomed triumph—the proclivity to win that is in David's nature and that brings him his loss.

X

The Enumerations

Building the Temple was David's idea.

Though eventually the construction will be left to his heir Solomon, at first it appears that David will himself build the project he conceives. As soon as the ark has come into the City of David, with David whirling in abandon at the head of the dancing procession, he declares that the Lord should have a house. This plan emerges immediately after David's argument with Michal about his dancing naked, their hateful exchange ending with the pronouncement that Michal will remain barren.

Michal will be barren, but David means to build. He says to Nathan the prophet, "See now, I dwell in an house of cedar, but the ark of God dwelleth within curtains."

And Nathan replies, "Go, do all that is in thine heart, for the Lord is with thee."

But Nathan has a vision that night. The Lord comes to him and emphatically yet obscurely postpones the Temple for a generation, while making David great promises:

"And it came to pass that night, that the word of the Lord

came unto Nathan, saying, Go and tell my servant David, Thus saith the Lord, Shalt thou build me an house for me to dwell in? Whereas I have not dwelt in any house since the time that I brought up the children of Israel out of Egypt, even to this day, but have walked in a tent and in a tabernacle. In all the places wherein I have walked with all the children of Israel spake I a word with any of the tribes of Israel, whom I commanded to feed my people Israel, saying, Why build ye not me an house of cedar?"

To this point, the Lord seems to disown David's idea of a house. It is too unheard-of, God seems to say. The Temple (which will indeed be built of cedar) would be a departure from the customary tabernacle of cloth and skins. But the Lord continues, and seems to accept that David's reign will transform the old days of wandering and dwelling in tents. When David rose from tending sheep to ruling Israel, the Lord indicates, he began a progression from tent to temple, from wandering to dwelling in an appointed place:

"Now therefore so shalt thou say unto my servant David, Thus saith the Lord of hosts, I took thee from the sheepcote, from following the sheep, to be ruler over my people, over Israel: And I was with thee whithersoever thou wentest, and have cut off all thine enemies out of thy sight, and have made thee a great name, like unto the name of the great men that are in the earth. Moreover I will appoint a place for my people Israel, and will plant them, that they may dwell in a place of their own, and move no more; neither shall the children of wickedness afflict them any more, as beforetime, and as since the time that I commanded judges to be over my people Israel, and have caused thee to rest from all thine enemies. Also the Lord telleth thee that he will make thee an house."

And the Lord's speech then turns in a nearly complete reversal of its beginning: the house of cedar is not rejected, or even disowned, but delayed for a generation:

"And when thy days be fulfilled, and thou shalt sleep with thy fathers, I will set up thy seed after thee, which shall proceed out of thy bowels, and I will establish his kingdom. He shall build an house for my name, and I will establish the throne of his kingdom for ever."

This peculiar matter of the Lord somehow accepting yet delaying the Temple registers the transforming, great political accomplishments of David as a ruler. It is as if God feels that David's changes can't be accepted too quickly, nearly as if David has taken divinity itself by surprise—David is in some sense too quick even for the Lord.

Ambivalence about David's reign, the way he changes everything, is embedded in the accounts of his glory, as in this peculiar episode of his desire to build the Lord a house. The Lord all but says, "No it is for *me* to create a house for *you*." Meanwhile, David reigns. His actual, historical government is visible, though beclouded by the gigantic, many-armed squid of two millennia, the successive passions and agendas of centuries.

This same sense that the Lord (or the narrative itself) is ambivalent about David's energy recurs later in David's career, with the command that David make a census. The command—"Go, number Israel and Judah"—is attributed to the Lord in the Book of Samuel 1:24:1; but in the Book of Chronicles 1:21:1, the words are differently attributed: "Satan stood up against Israel and incited David to number Israel."

The difference in meaning created by the Chronicler substituting "Satan" for "the Lord" is not so stark as it seems—because in the Book of Samuel, the Lord's motives are not benign: "Again the anger of the Lord was kindled against Israel, and he incited David against them, saying, Go, number Israel and Judah." And in all tellings Joab, when David commands him to conduct a census by using the army, protests—the commander finding the king's plan objectionable in both accounts, whether incited by Satan or by a wrathful God. Joab's reasons for resisting the enumeration, like David's reasons for ordering it, are vague.

Or, "vague" is an understatement. What is so bad about the census? The English *census*—like English *censorious* and *censor*—comes from a Roman public office, an official note that chimes with dread of officialdom, the surnames imposed on European Jews by Imperial or imperious tax collectors, the fearsome rolls of cannon-fodder to be tormented, maimed or killed in the Czar's or the Emperor's army. But the Hebrew indicates counting, enumeration. And David's counting comes millennia before any Roman or Holy Roman or Czarist enumerations. Those are irrelevant, as are the more benign jokes and humiliations of Ellis Island officials. Why is the census denounced and then renounced, and why is the story told in a blur?

Scholarly explanations fumble among theories: "cultic"

taboos against counting; or a popular fear of taxes; or an association of the census with a military draft. None of these learned speculations is adequate to the idea of the census as Satanic, as in the Book of Chronicles. And the census does lead directly to a kind of Hell: a plague that continues until the Lord himself repents of it, after it has caused tens of thousands of deaths, with the enumeration of the deaths—"there died of the people from Dan even to Beersheba seventy thousand men"—itself a kind of paradox, since it is a counting of the dead.

David first wants the census, with no apparent motive, and then he begs pardon for wanting it—with as little reason for the contrition as there was for the undertaking. The Lord first behaves enigmatically, and then what we would call churlishly or crazily in anyone but a deity. And after all that, the abrupt denouement is as illogical as the beginning is blurry.

But the blur itself becomes a background that makes the outline of David sharper. Why might the quick youth, the skilled guerilla fighter, the great poet, the royal adulterer, the heartbroken father, the uniter of kingdoms, undertake a census? Why might he be portrayed as then lamenting his own undertaking, as a capricious ruler subject to an equally capricious deity?

Possibly because the uniter of the kingdom, the poet, the victorious and quick-witted and imperfect ruler, represents and executes a profound change: the transformation from a masked, uncataloged, exclusionary, taboo-ridden culture of tribes to a visible, enumerated, inclusive civilization—

embodied in the City of David, and affirmed in the act of tabulation by that central authority. That is, because the census is consistent with the rapid movement from tabernacle to Temple. The uneasy vagueness registers change, the unsettling blur of speed.

As the founding of Jerusalem extends David's enterprising, central magnetic character to the palpable kingdom, in the realm of stone and wood and brass, the census extends that same character into the realm of intelligence. The blur in the telling manifests anxiety about the fact that David seems to change the very nature of the Hebrews, indeed their very way of dealing with the Lord. As King Saul did not, as King Solomon will not, King David changes the world.

The issue raised or embodied by the census is not narrowly religious—manifesting God's anger or Satan's deception, with David a wooden pawn—but rather, political and in some way theological: for David's successes as king transform the metaphysical nature of things. His centralizing accomplishments throw a shadow over the old tribal leadership, the old notion of prophets—even the old functions of tabernacle and ark. The David who first conceives the Temple also creates a new political realm and new ways of being, in a single historical imagining.

David's diplomatic marriages and his military victories brought about a kind of empire, a consolidated area under his rule said to extend from the Euphrates to the Nile, and encompassing various nations and tribes. From Jerusalem, the City of David, he established an army and a court and a class of functionaries all belonging to the capital and to no tribe. Some were from Hebrew tribes, some from other tribes, but now they represented the king, in the City of David. King Saul exerted his authority by showing the hacked-apart team of oxen; King David's authority is manifest in the city he founds, and in the Temple imagined by David and constructed by his son King Solomon.

Such changes cannot go unresisted. When the poltroon Sheba son of Bichri begins his rebellion, he has some success because the rebel cry, shouted in response to the trumpet, arouses the old tribal loyalty: "We have no part in David, and neither have we inheritance in the son of Jesse: every man to his tents, O Israel." Sheba is from the tribe of Benjamin, like Saul, but the point is not loyalty to Benjamites, still less to the House of Saul—but an appeal to the idea of *tribe*, itself: "Every man to his tents." Identifying David as "the son of Jesse" is an attempt to reduce him back to his origins, and to ignore the new reality of Jerusalem. The City of David, wrested away from the Jebusites who were in the land before any tribe of the Philistines or the Hebrews, belongs to no tribe and is rejected by those who rally back to their tents.

In the narrative of Saul and David and the many secondary characters around them, people are often identified by tribe rather than nation or religion; and sometimes it is not easy for the casual reader to detect if some personage's tribe is Hebrew or Philistine or Canaanite. This idea of tribe, less bodily and evident than family, more inward and enduring than hometown, is not easy to imagine for us who live out-

side of the concept. Even the word "kin" has an archaic fla-
vor in modern life, and we hardly recognize kin's companion
"kith," which besides meaning "the known" also means "the
properly-behaving": it is the same word as "couth." Members of a tribe are likely to share not only kinship but kith: a
knowing and a behaving; a system of identity, not of government; a system judging what is uncouth or "unheard of"
rather than what is illegal.

The tribe involves consanguinity but not necessarily
family; nativity but not necessarily native land or any
other geography; authority but not necessarily government.
It might resemble regionalism, but with no emphasis on
region—as though Southerners were a blood-bonded entity
without reference to the South, or New Englanders without
New England. Or maybe it is closer to a city sense of the
Magyar or Korean or Dominican neighborhood, but again
with no unalterable attachment to the real estate of that
particular block. In the workplace or social gathering or worship, or even in a marriage, one person might be Magyar or
Southern and the other New Englander or Korean, and the
marriage or friendship or enmity or collegiality might possibly override the tribal distinction of the Southern-ness on
one side and the Korean-ness on the other—but not obliterate it.

The analogies are worthwhile only negatively, by their
inadequacy. They remind us not to assume religion or nation
as the root of passions that may be tribal. The prophet
Samuel's elaborate warning about the king he is about to
select and anoint, because the Lord is giving the people what

they want—like an irritated, misgiving parent—may have to do with kings *versus* prophets or judges, or with a central king *versus* his individual subjects, but it surely has to do with the ways of a king *versus* the old way of tribes, as well.

The weird and weirdly elusive episode of King David and the census recalls that speech of Samuel's, on the subject of kings, addressed to the people before the prophet sets out to find and anoint Saul. Samuel's rhetoric itself is richly enumerative and detailed. It is worth repeating:

"This will be the manner of the king that shall reign over you: He will take your sons, and appoint them for himself, for his chariots, and to be his horsemen; and some shall run before his chariots. And he will appoint him captains over thousands, and captains over fifties; and will set them to ear his ground, and to reap his harvest, and to make his instruments of war, and instruments of his chariots. And he will take your daughters to be confectionaries, and to be cooks, and to be bakers. And he will take your fields, and your vineyards, and your oliveyards, even the best of them, and give them to his servants. And he will take the tenth of your seed, and of your vineyards, and give to his officers, and to his servants. And he will take your menservants, and your maidservants, and your goodliest young men, and your asses, and put them to his work. He will take the tenth of your sheep: and ye shall be his servants. And ye shall cry out in that day because of your king which ye shall have chosen you; and the Lord will not hear you in that day."

A remarkable speech from the very man who is about to anoint the new king—but the rhetoric does not persuade them: "Nevertheless the people refused to obey the voice of Samuel; and they said, Nay; but we will have a king over us."

The Lord dictates the anti-monarchical speech to Samuel with a remarkably negative proviso: "Hearken to the voice of the people in all that they say to you; for they have not rejected you, but they have rejected me from being king over them. According to all the deeds which they have done to me, from the day I brought them up out of Egypt even to this day, forsaking me and serving other gods, so they are also doing to you. Now then, hearken to their voice; only, you shall solemnly warn them, and show them the ways of the king who shall reign over them."

This giving accompanied by a deprecation of the gift—and deprecation moreover in great detail—is perhaps strange theologically. It is certainly strange as the divine justification for a dynasty. (The interrupting sentence about Egypt, and serving other gods, appears to be added by the "Deuteronomist," ineffectively rationalizing the Lord's ambiguous granting of a king.)

Long before David is urged to number the people, whether by Satan or by a God punishing offenses against him by urging a further offense, Samuel the anointing but displeased prophet catalogs the drawbacks of kingship. Why did the people originally request a king? Because Samuel had appointed his corrupt, venal sons as judges. A judge's authority may rest partly on an appointing prophet, but it must rest also on his day-to-day reputation for justice. Two tribesmen who have a dispute may come before a judge as though before a civil court; so too may an entire community or part of the community—every man from his tents, consulting the judge for a specific ruling, but not for rule. The authority of the king—Saul sending those oxen parts around the country, or David making Jerusalem his capital—has a different, established status. The king too is anointed by religious authorities, but the king rules, with his authority resting on power as demonstrated by his ability to slaughter your livestock, to build a city—or, it may be, to enumerate his subjects by census.

This difference between old ways and new enables the rebellion of Absalom, and explains why some brief success comes even to the rebellion incited by the "worthless fellow" Sheba, with his cry of *"Every man to his tents."* The cry has a stupendous power, imaginative and practical. The tabernacle itself is a tent, or anyway a frail hut or booth, of boards and poles, with walls of animal skin, woven goat-hair and embroidered linen—the very word in English a close relative of "tavern." When dancing David brings the holy ark into his city, the wild procession with the ark behind him takes its ecstatic course away from the tribal tents and toward a centralizing, literal architecture—permanent, or if not exactly permanent then built to last. The inner energy that drives the naked king as he spins through the streets leading the procession of the ark will also send his officers through the country, to conduct the census. The ultimate riposte to Samuel's sour description of the king, and the ultimate triumph over Sheba of Bichri's slogan "Every man to his tents," will be embodied by David's heir: Solomon, the first to inherit the kingship, and a builder as well as a poet.

What Solomon completes, in the elaborately splendid First Temple with its adjoining royal palace, is perhaps less a sacred shrine or a nation than the true opposite of a tribe: a city. The *polis* offers a structure of identity that challenges or effaces the old private and by definition clannish identity of tents, chieftains and patterns of connection, embodied not by measurable and countable walls or roadways but by blood and kith. In that world of the tents, apparently, one may be permitted to count foreskins of the dead—but not living souls.

When David dies, the narration is strikingly terse: one sentence. Whereas David sings his great elegies for Saul and Jonathan and for Joab, we have no dirge or lament for David, even though his son Solomon is also credited with great poetry. Solomon's equivalent of an elegy for David is his building the City of David. Not only the Temple but the very description of the Temple is a hymn to David, and to the civic aspect of his career, cloaked in the peculiar business of numbering Israel and Judah.

When David in the spirit of the *polis*, satanic or divine, commands a census, Joab in the spirit of the tents protests; but he reluctantly obeys David. Joab has his officers count the population, a methodical survey of the empire that takes nine months. The result is not only male and adult, but military: "and there were in Israel eight hundred thousand valiant men that drew the sword; and the men of Judah were five hundred thousand men." Immediately, "David's heart smote him," and he confesses to the Lord—the very God who told him to count the people, unless it was Satan—"I have sinned greatly in that I have done: and now I beseech thee, O Lord, take away the iniquity of thy servant: for I have done very foolishly."

This mechanical reversal by David, manifesting a profound cultural ambivalence, meets an equally irrational response from the Lord, who tells his prophet, Gad:

"Go and say unto David, Thus saith the Lord, I offer thee three things; choose one of them, that I may do it unto thee."

So David gets the following three choices from the Lord's prophet:

"Shall seven years of famine come unto thee in thy land? Or wilt thou flee three months before thine enemies, while they pursue thee? Or that there be three days' pestilence in thy land? now advise, and see what answer I shall return to him that sent me."

The three choices resemble a folktale, but a very unsatisfying folktale. What follows lacks narrative logic, but retains the character of David's intelligence: confronted with the three punishments, instead of choosing David makes an answer that both flatters the Lord and puts the weight of choice back on the Lord. David says:

"I am in a great strait: let us fall now into the hand of the Lord; for his mercies are great: and let me not fall into the hand of man."

This recalls the poetic voice that soothed Saul. On a religious level, David's resourceful answer contains a formula—the wish to fall into the hands of God rather than of man—that is repeated every day by observant Jews who recite the penitential blessing. It is as though David the artist (metrical poetry and music, like the census, involve numbers) shines through the mist of a faulty, anxious narrative—the story itself terrified that its dynamic protagonist, with his making of poems and cities and music and enumerations, will bend or break the frame of God's will—David making a phrase that will be uttered daily for millennia.

On a narrative level, David's answer, excluding pursuit by the human enemy, ought to leave a choice between the divine visitations of famine and pestilence; however, the next sentence is:

"So the Lord sent a pestilence upon Israel from the morning even to the time appointed: and there died of the people even from Dan to Beersheba seventy thousand men." David's succinct, canny preference for the hand of the Lord over the hand of men has his shrewdness. But the flubbed syllogism of the outcome is disappointing—why should it be the Lord who chooses between famine and pestilence?—making the disproportionate death of seventy thousand all the more terrible and opaque, and all the less a demonstration of mercy from the hand of God.

And the seventy thousand are enumerated, as though the story needs to turn against itself yet again: the putative later hands, with their religious purpose, making a narrative that stings itself in the tail, by counting the dead who died as retribution for counting the living. Behind the shadowy, uncertain contest between God and David, or between Satan and David, perhaps behind the notion that counting has an ancient superstitious ban against it, or incorporating that notion, is a real, and precisely *political* contest. The contest is between, on one side, the spirit of enumeration—which is the spirit of the royal capital, the *polis* with its shifting, diverse population and official life—and on the other side, that ancient tribal spirit of every man with his private tents, where the cry is, "We have no part in David, and neither have we inheritance in the son of Jesse."

The construction executed by Hiram of Tyre for David's inheritor Solomon is presented in a visionary, extended catalog, full of enumerations. Visionary of divinity maybe, but certainly visionary of enumerated and specified splendor, like Solomon's personal accomplishments. Solomon, says the Book of Kings, spoke three thousand proverbs and composed one thousand and five songs. "And he spake of trees, from the cedar tree that is in Lebanon even unto the hyssop that springeth out of the wall: he spake also of beasts, and of fowl, and of creeping things, and of fishes." He is the alleged author of the canonical "Song of Solomon" and of apocryphal Psalms and Odes. His wisdom excelled the wisdom of all the children of the East, and all the wisdom of Egypt.

But it is for a palpable, glorious flowering of matter, manufactured and graven and civilized, that Solomon is celebrated most elaborately. The passages specifying and exemplifying Solomon's wisdom are briefer than the prolonged, detailed, lyrical enumeration of the palace and Temple built for Solomon by Hiram of Tyre. Not only the structures of cedar and fir, the costly stones and extensive brasswork, accomplished by ten thousand laborers and eighty carvers. Also the specific numbers and dimensions of windows, doors of olivewood, the detailed architectural ornaments and floor-plan, the ornaments, the sheathing of gold, the five-cubit cherubim of carved olivewood and the palm trees also carved of olivewood, the porch of judgment with Solomon's throne, and another porch for his wife Pharaoh's daughter, brass pillars and brass checker-work and net-work and lily-work, carved and cast animals and plants, identified and enumerated, and ornamental wheels all of brass, with their specific dimensions as well.

The great "molten sea" or pool for the priests to bathe in, with its brim outcurved like a lily, is supported on the radial backs of twelve sculpted oxen or bulls, facing outward. Four hundred symmetrical cast pomegranates. Also recorded are implements and vessels: pots and shovels and basins; ewers, lampstands, the show-bread table of gold—which will be depicted in bas-relief, along with the branched candlesticks, a thousand years later on the triumphal arch in the Roman Forum, celebrating the capture and destruction of Jerusalem by the Emperor Titus.

The enumeration and description have the obsessive quality of Robinson Crusoe's lists, or manic writing about sex or food. (Readers of American poetry will recognize a note of exquisite, compulsive specificity struck by James McMichael's description of Pasadena houses.) Here is a sample of the lyrical catalog of Solomon's palace and Temple, arranged in strophes. The quotation must be extended, because sheer volume is germane to the matter of the census (a "chapter" is the capital finishing off the top of a column):

And nets of checker work, and wreaths of chain work, for the chapiters which were upon the top of the pillars; seven for the one chapiter, and seven for the other chapiter.

And he made the pillars, and two rows round about upon the one network, to cover the chapiters that were upon the top, with pomegranates: and so did he for the other chapiter.

And the chapiters that were upon the top of the pillars were of lily work in the porch, four cubits.

And the chapiters upon the two pillars had pomegranates also above, over against the belly which was by the network: and the pomegranates were two hundred in rows round about upon the other chapiter.

Hiram also built the "molten sea" where the priests were to bathe. (A "knop" is a gourd or knob.)

And he made a molten sea, ten cubits from the one brim to the other: it was round all about, and his height was five cubits: and a line of thirty cubits did compass it round about.

And under the brim of it round about there were knops compassing it, ten in a cubit, compassing the sea round about: the knops were cast in two rows, when it was cast.

It stood upon twelve oxen, three looking toward the
  north, and three looking toward the west, and
  three looking toward the south, and three looking
  toward the east: and the sea was set above upon
  them, and all their hinder parts were inward.

And it was an hand breadth thick, and the brim
  thereof was wrought like the brim of a cup, with
  flowers of lilies: it contained two thousand baths.

Lilies, pomegranates, lions, the concentric oxen looking outward, supporting the great "sea" or pool, and along with the
imagery of splendor, emerging through translation, a luxuri-
ance, even magnificence, of technical nomenclature. Here is
building, and description of building, that glorifies the Lord,
but that also celebrates the palpable, intricate and massive
work of a civilized capital, with its cosmopolitan arts and
industries:

And the work of the bases was on this manner: they
  had borders, and the borders were between the
  ledges:

And on the borders that were between the ledges were
  lions, oxen, and cherubims: and upon the ledges
  there was a base above: and beneath the lions and
  oxen were certain additions made of thin work.

And every base had four brasen wheels, and plates of
  brass: and the four corners thereof had

undersetters: under the laver were undersetters molten, at the side of every addition.

And the mouth of it within the chapiter and above was a cubit: but the mouth thereof was round after the work of the base, a cubit and an half: and also upon the mouth of it were gravings with their borders, foursquare, not round.

And under the borders were four wheels; and the axletrees of the wheels were joined to the base: and the height of a wheel was a cubit and half a cubit.

And the work of the wheels was like the work of a chariot wheel: their axletrees, and their naves, and their felloes, and their spokes, were all molten.

And there were four undersetters to the four corners of one base: and the undersetters were of the very base itself.

This is a long way from the portable tabernacle, with its walls of badger-skin and linen. The distance is in the enumerations, and the proliferation of images, as well as in the materials. Such profusion of brazen or gilded oxen and pomegranates and wheels, in the image-language of a film set, would indicate something pagan or decadent. The ornaments and their verbal description, both, have an ebullient quality of art: the power to create, celebrating itself. David takes up the harp and raises his voice to memorialize his predecessor Saul. No poet-musician is required to memorialize David in a parallel way. His greatness as a king, and his creation of the idea of the kingship infinitely extended, are instead celebrated by this extended anthem of splendor—David's idea brought into being by David's son and successor: the Temple in the City of David, with its artful and enumerated lions, cherubim, palm trees, knops, chapiters, lily-work and checker-work. And as if in additional memorial tribute to the poet David the Jews live and worship not in this or any extant Temple but in this constructed description of the Temple.

XI

I Will Make Thine
Enemies Thy Footstool

N ow king David was old and stricken in years; and they
covered him with clothes, but he gat no heat."

Such is the first verse of the Book of the Kings, the clini-
cal outright statement increasing the awful weight of it. The
youth who staggered under Saul's armor, who exchanged
clothes with Jonathan, who doubled the bride price of a hundred foreskins, the man who won Abigail and Bathsheba and
danced naked before the ark, eyed by Michal and the servant
girls, the supreme poet and general, the maker of Jerusalem,
the city he lost and regained—cannot get warm. As when he
first grows faint in battle, and needs to be rescued from the
giant cousin or nephew of Goliath, this debility seems to
violate David's nature. And as with that growing faint in
battle against the giant, his nature eventually incorporates
the weakness, too—in a sense masters it.

It is an essential part of David's meaning that he is visible
at so many stages of life. Not for David to die young like
Achilles, nor to endure old age offstage and out of our sight

like Odysseus, nor to go down as a grizzled warrior like Beowulf charging into the cold twilight a final time to kill and die for his people. Lear may have been a beautiful boy once, but that is left to idle imagining—in the neverland where we are free to imagine Romeo and Juliet, had things gone differently, as a mellow old couple. Not for David the avenging self-destruction of Samson, nor the conclusive Pisgah vision of Moses, who is seen from childhood to old age but not in fulfillment. David's drama is that of a life entire. David in his faults and attainments, his losses and victories, embodies on a scale almost beyond imagining the action of *living a life.*

In a midrash recounted by Ginzberg, David was originally destined by the Lord to die in infancy. But in the region of Paradise where souls can be viewed before they are born, Adam beheld the soul of David and recognized a quality that moved him to make a remarkable proposition to God.

"Lord," said the father of all people, "this comely soul should have a life longer than a few days or weeks. You have allotted me a thousand years of life on earth. Let me give seventy of them to David."

So the Lord of hosts has his angels draw up a contract, specifying in writing that Adam the undersigned does yield and assign seventy of his thousand years to the forenamed recipient David son of Jesse. And Adam signs the contract, giving David the prescribed, lifetime-epitomizing three score and ten. The daffy element of legalism, the binding document signed by all parties, recognizes from afar a profound, inclusive worldliness—as though, for the brilliant and God-haunted bookworm who dreamed this myth, the sensual or busy world outside the studyhouse, the world of David, would be epitomized by the worldliness of a legal contract.

Adam, the progenitor who contains all human attributes, recognizes in the infant soul of David his future epitome, transformed from everyman to a quintessence: a superman, if that term includes super-concentrated human failings. As Adam the created contains like a seedpod all human qualities in their first state, David the beloved unfolds the dream of all those qualities realized and violently flowered into action, earthly yet ultimate.

He endures and overcomes whatever tries to pull him down at each stage of life: the upstart lad's dismissal by elders and superiors; the endangered youth's contest with authority that is capriciously malign and affectionate; the mature man's struggle for conquest or subjugation; the ambitious man's exacting wiles, including feigned insanity and juggled loyalties and ruthless violence and reckless seduction and vengeance foregone. He survives the self-injuring lust of middle age; he endures the guilts and regrets of fatherhood, with the rape of Tamar leading to the loss of Amnon, and the consequent loss of Absalom a wound to the father David inflicted by David's own power and will—David suffering all to triumph over all, as he must now suffer, and triumph over, not only the weaknesses of age, but gigantic death itself, by extending his will beyond the grave.

So David must be, among other things—among all things—old. And enfeebled, too. But he is still the king;

and though the courtiers' suggestion for dealing with his condition may have been discussed among his counselors and family, it is narrated as a proposal made to the king, for David himself to accept or not:

"Wherefore his servants said unto him, Let there be sought for my lord the king a young virgin: and let her stand before the king, and let her cherish him, and let her lie in thy bosom, that my lord the king may get heat."

The "servants"—courtiers, politicians and family members—doubtless have each of them their own personal motives, factions, alliances, as well as concern for the king. Who will succeed him? Who will gain and who will lose? In the court as in the family, love and gain, loyalty and conspiracy, come in braided strands, not easily identified by the participants themselves. Love and power, loyalty and gain, swirl around their cooling focus, the king. When the servants of David present this plan to him, he apparently assents, or even approves:

"So they sought for a fair damsel throughout all the coasts of Israel, and found Abishag a Shunamite, and brought her to the king. And the damsel was very fair, and ministered to him: but the king knew her not."

The story's triple linking of beauty, old age and worldly ambition communicated itself to Robert Frost, who begins his poem "Provide, Provide" with a reference to Abishag:

> The witch that came (the withered hag)
> To wash the steps with pail and rag
> Was once the beauty Abishag,

> The picture pride of Hollywood.
> Too many fall from great and good
> For you to doubt the likelihood.

"If need be acquire a throne," Frost says a few lines later, "Where nobody can call *you* crone." Frost's brilliant lines are like a wistful, comic reflection of the monumental view of human age delivered by the supreme poetry of Psalm 90, comparing a human span of time to the Lord's eternity:

> Before the mountains were brought forth, or ever thou
>   hadst formed the earth and the world, even from
>   everlasting to everlasting, thou art God.

> Thou turnest man to destruction; and sayest, Return,
>   ye children of men.

> For a thousand years in thy sight are but as yesterday
>   when it is past, and as a watch in the night.

> Thou carriest them away as with a flood; they are as a
>   sleep: in the morning they are like grass which
>   groweth up.

> In the morning it flourisheth, and groweth up; in the
>   evening it is cut down, and withereth.

> For we are consumed by thine anger, and by thy wrath
>   are we troubled.

Thou hast set our iniquities before thee, our secret
    sins in the light of thy countenance.

For all our days are passed away in thy wrath: we
    spend our years as a tale that is told.

The days of our years are threescore years and ten;
    and if by reason of strength they be fourscore
    years, yet is their strength labour and sorrow; for it
    is soon cut off, and we fly away.

To imagine these lines as composed by David himself (tradition calls Psalm 90 "a prayer of Moses") is to feel an additional authority and pathos in *we spend our years as a tale that is told*. No life ever was more like a tale than David's, but it too spends itself like a narrative trickling or unwinding away into God's eternity, in whose wrath we pass away our days. Frost's lines are a sardonic, American midrash on the theme.

Adonijah, the next eldest son after Absalom, also is an impressive-looking man, and like Absalom he gets chariots for himself, and horsemen, and fifty attendants to run before him. About Adonijah's character and behavior the narrative is even more explicit than about Absalom: "he exalted himself, saying, I will be king." And, regarding Adonijah in relation to his father David: "And his father had not displeased him at any time by saying, Why hast thou done so?"

So Adonijah is an indulged son never contradicted, the eldest now with Absalom dead; and logically enough, as the time for succession approaches, Adonijah attracts the sup port and counsel of Joab, commander of the army. Abiathar the priest also joins the faction of the apparent heir. "And they following Adonijah helped him." Possibly guided by Abiathar and Joab, Adonijah has a great gathering at a site a little outside Jerusalem, to which he invites all his brothers (except Solomon), and his counselors the general and the priest, along with "all the royal officials of Judah." At this occasion, before the eyes of those he has invited, Adonijah takes it upon himself to perform the ritual sacrifices "of sheep, oxen and fatlings"—as though he had already inherited. Another faction is not invited:

"But Nathan the prophet, and Benaiah, and the mighty men, and Solomon his brother, he called not. Wherefore Nathan spake unto Bathsheba the mother of Solomon, saying, Hast thou not heard that Adonijah the son of Haggith doth reign, and David knoweth it not."

The prophet Nathan who denounced David for murdering Uriah the Hittite and taking Bathsheba now is Bathsheba's ally. He says to her:

"Now therefore come, let me, I pray thee, give thee counsel, that thou mayest save thine own life, and the life of thy son Solomon. Go and get thee in unto king David, and say unto him, Didst not thou, my lord, O king, swear unto thine handmaid, saying, Assuredly Solomon thy son shall reign after me, and he shall sit upon my throne? why then doth Adonijah reign? Behold, while thou yet talkest there with the king, I also will come in after thee, and confirm thy words."

Nathan's last sentence to Bathsheba here raises the possibility that this reminder of a promise is a deception: if David made the promise to Bathsheba that Solomon should rule, why need corroboration from Nathan? Or, the promise was indeed made but possibly not announced or disseminated. In any case, Bathsheba, in that line of women who after seeming passive show their unanticipated strength, follows Nathan's counsel:

"And Bathsheba went in unto the king into the chamber; and the king was very old; and Abishag the Shunamite ministered unto the king. And Bathsheba bowed, and did obeisance unto the king. And the king said, What wouldest thou?"

The woman David long ago, fresh from his nap, saw from the rooftop while she bathed, in the time after the soldiers first told him he could no longer risk actual combat, does obeisance before him as an old man. Now it is clear that Bathsheba is younger than David (though not as young as Abishag). Bathsheba says to David:

"My lord, thou swarest by the Lord thy God unto thine handmaid, saying, Assuredly Solomon thy son shall reign after me, and he shall sit upon my throne. And now, behold, Adonijah reigneth; and now, my lord the king, thou knowest it not: and he hath slain oxen and fat cattle and sheep in abundance, and hath called all the sons of the king, and Abiathar the priest, and Joab the captain of the host: but Solomon thy servant hath he not called. And thou, my lord, O king, the eyes of all Israel are upon thee, that thou shouldest tell them who shall sit on the throne of my lord the king after him. Otherwise it shall come to pass, when my lord the king sleeps with his fathers, that I and my son Solomon shall be counted offenders."

Bathsheba in this speech unexpectedly but maybe cunningly puts David's promise at its beginning, building toward the information, perhaps more moving to the king, that Adonijah "reigneth" and that the eyes of all Israel wait to see what David will do. Adonijah's presumption and the nation's attention may be more persuasive than the promise, fabricated or genuine. And at the climax of Bathsheba's words to David, "My son Solomon and I shall be counted offenders." The idea that David will be unable to save the "offenders" from being killed may be Bathsheba's crowning argument: it is in David's power now to save Bathsheba and Solomon the blameless, as he could not save Absalom the rebel, and before that could not save Amnon the rapist. (And long before that, he could not save, though he fasted and tore his clothing and prayed, his first child with this woman.)

According to plan, after Bathsheba has said these words about David's promise, and the eyes of Israel watching him, and the threat to herself and Solomon, Nathan the prophet enters the bedchamber. He bows, and puts his face to the ground—like Bathsheba, Nathan observing throne-room formality here at the bedside, though she has shared David's bed and Nathan has denounced him for it—and addresses the king:

"And Nathan said, My lord, O king, hast thou said, Adonijah shall reign after me, and he shall sit upon my throne? For he is gone down this day, and hath slain oxen and fat cattle and sheep in abundance, and hath called all the king's sons, and the captains of the host, and Abiathar the priest; and, behold, they eat and drink before him, and say, God save king Adonijah. But me, even me thy servant, and Zadok the priest, and Benaiah the son of Jehoiada, and thy servant Solomon, hath he not called. Is this thing done by my lord the king, and thou hast not shewed it unto thy servant, who should sit on the throne of my lord the king after him?"

Bathsheba and Nathan stake everything on the appeal to David's authority. On some level, they are inviting him to be David: that is, not only to determine how things will be, and not only to enforce his will upon events, but to upset and contradict the apparent and apparently official and ordained nature of events. Against Adonijah's ceremonious feast, with the sacrifices and royal officials of Judah, the princely sons and the commander Joab and the priest Abiathar, against even the plausible if not mandatory principle of primogeniture, against the fact that Adonijah is not only older than Solomon but has halfway or more actually succeeded to the throne—against all of that, Nathan and Bathsheba counterpose David's own will.

And perhaps his word. But in either case, it is David pitted against that gathering a bit outside of the city, with its splendid sacrifices, and feasting, and the equivalent of toasts and speeches. It is as though for David this is a final opportunity to be the confident underdog, upsetting the foregone conclusion and defying the challenges of the mighty. That gathering of princes and dignitaries, celebrating by a spring outside town, is in some way like the older brothers or the giant or the established order. He can again not only thwart priests and generals but astound them. In any case, when Nathan has made his case, David responds with his old crisp insight and command. He remains the Lord's anointed winner:

"Then king David answered and said, Call me Bathsheba. And she came into the king's presence, and stood before the king. And the king sware, and said, As the Lord liveth, that hath redeemed my soul out of all distress, even as I sware unto thee by the Lord God of Israel, saying, Assuredly Solomon thy son shall reign after me, and he shall sit upon my throne in my stead; even so will I certainly do this day."

"In my stead" and "this day": this goes further than Bathsheba and Nathan have asked. Solomon will become King of Israel and Judah at once, today. It may be with genuine awe, as well as whatever irony, that Bathsheba in response again bows, with her face to the earth—Abishag the Shunamite presumably standing by—and says, "Let my Lord king David live for ever." Awe is due to how the old king demonstrates that he has a plan; and can name those who will execute it; and chooses to specify how they will carry it out for him:

"And king David said, Call me Zadok the priest, and Nathan the prophet, and Benaiah the son of Jehoiada. And they came before the king. The king also said unto them, Take with you the servants of your lord, and cause Solomon my son to ride upon mine own mule, and bring him down to Gihon: and let Zadok the priest and Nathan the prophet anoint him there king over Israel: and blow ye with the trumpet, and say, God save king Solomon. Then ye shall come up after him, that he may come and sit upon my throne; for he shall be king in my stead: and I have appointed him to be ruler over Israel and over Judah."

Just as David instructs, Zadok the priest and Nathan the prophet and Benaiah, with those loyal Philistine troops the Cherethites and the Pelethites, accompany Solomon mounted on David's mule to Gihon, within earshot of Adonijah's party. There, Zadok the priest anoints Solomon with oil from the tabernacle. With the anointing, blasts on the trumpet, and shouts by the people of "God save king Solomon!"

To counter Adonijah's sacrifices, an anointing; to counter his gathering, a parade, including the royal mule; to counter his distinguished guest list, the Cherethites and the Pelethites and "the people" shouting. This counter-ceremony has its effect:

"And all the people came up after him, and the people piped with pipes, and rejoiced with great joy, so that the earth rent with the sound of them. And Adonijah and all the guests that were with him heard it as they had made an end of eating. And when Joab heard the sound of the trumpet, he said, Wherefore is this noise of the city being in an uproar?"

Joab, not Adonijah, asks this question, indicating that the army commander may sense what is happening—maybe that Joab has been as much Adonijah's instigator as his counselor. But it is to Adonijah that the report is delivered by the priest's son Jonathan. The report, repeating what has already been narrated, resembles the refrain of a poem—the poem of old David's new victory:

"And Jonathan answered and said to Adonijah: Verily our lord king David hath made Solomon king. And the king hath sent with him Zadok the priest, and Nathan the prophet, and Benaiah the son of Jehoiada, and the Cherethites, and the Pelethites, and they have caused him to ride upon the king's mule. And Zadok the priest and Nathan the prophet have anointed him king in Gihon: and they are come up from thence rejoicing, so that the city rang again. This is the noise that ye have heard. And also Solomon sitteth on the throne of the kingdom."

And as if that were not enough:

"And moreover the king's servants came to bless our lord king David, saying God make the name of Solomon better than thy name, and make his throne greater than thy throne. And the king bowed himself upon the bed. And also thus said the king, Blessed be the Lord God of Israel, which hath given one to sit on my throne this day, mine eyes even seeing it."

David's triumph, celebrated by the formulaic blessing that one's dynastic heirs will exceed even one's own greatness—representing in its way the largest and most subtle congratulation a patriarch can receive—is complete. Adonijah's guests, in fear, rise and leave, "every man his way." And the prince Adonijah himself knows that he is in danger, and seeks sanctuary. Now we must hear the voice of Solomon, confronted with his first challenge as king:

"And Adonijah feared because of Solomon, and arose, and went, and caught hold on the horns of the altar. And it was told Solomon, saying Behold, Adonijah feareth king Solomon: for lo, he hath caught hold on the horns of the altar, saying,

Let king Solomon swear unto me to day that he will not slay his servant with the sword."

Adonijah relies for his life upon the surrender in the words "his servant" and upon the idea that one should not kill a man gripping the horns—four projections upturned from the corners—of the altar. And David's intention to create a dynasty depends upon how Solomon deals with the situation. Solomon's message to his brother Adonijah has the subtlety and authority, and maybe the menace, of their father:

"And Solomon said, If he will shew himself a worthy man, there shall be not an hair of him fall to the earth: but if wickedness shall be found in him, he shall die. So king Solomon sent, and they brought him down from the altar. And he came and bowed himself to king Solomon: and Solomon said unto him, Go to thine house."

That Adonijah is spared amplifies the victory of David, who from his deathbed has not only appointed the one son his heir but has for now saved the other son's life. The dynastic survival is established not only literally by Solomon's accession but in spirit by the manifestation of David in Solomon's voice. The terse "Go to thine house" leaves no doubt who is in charge, and circumscribes the life—private and domestic—assigned to the bowing Adonijah.

Nor is that David's final victory on earth. He calls Solomon to him, saying, "I go the way of all the earth," and proceeds to give terse, expert instructions about the disposition of worldly matters. Worldly, and also political, as well as bloodstained. The gangster analogy is impossible to avoid:

David, with his mind full of cunning, venom and purpose, even as he leaves the world, says to Solomon:

"Moreover thou knowest also what Joab the son of Zeruiah did to me, and what he did to the two captains of the hosts of Israel, unto Abner the son of Ner, and unto Amasa the son of Jether, whom he slew, and shed the blood of war in peace, and put the blood of war upon his girdle that was about his loins, and in his shoes that were on his feet. Do therefore according to thy wisdom, and let not his hoar head go down to the grave in peace."

The nastiness of David's last formula, which wills Solomon to send Joab's gray head down in gore and pain, may be mitigated by the many years David has needed to deal gently with the dangerous old general and his bloody deeds. Joab stabbed Abner for vendetta and Amasa for rivalry, and neither one in the course of war—as he killed Absalom—but pretending friendship, embracing his victims so that their blood spattered his garments, just as David says. Abner and Amasa, who had been David's opponents in war, died at Joab's hand not in battle but by treachery.

But David's instructions about Joab's hoar head are shocking nonetheless. In contrast, David instructs Solomon to show kindness to the sons of old Barzillai the loyal Gileadite "who came to me when I fled because of Absalom thy brother." This reward and Joab's death sentence both indicate David's vigorous interest not simply in settling scores but in seeing the end of life as definitive, with old age and death as the significant registers of a life—the final score.

These deeply secular, power-conscious, nearly thuggish

last instructions are given comical emphasis by an interpolation by the much later, pious author-editor called "the Deuteronomist"—an anachronistic command to study and obey Deuteronomy. The transition is so abrupt, and such a reversal, that if we accept the words as spoken by David, the effect is of a perfunctory, hypocritical preamble to the real business:

"I go the way of all the earth: be thou strong therefore, and shew thyself a man; And keep the charge of the Lord thy God, to walk in his ways, to keep his statutes, and his commandments, and his judgments, and his testimonies, as it is written in the law of Moses, that thou mayest prosper in all that thou doest, and whithersoever thou turnest thyself: That the Lord may continue his word which he spake concerning me, saying, If thy children take heed to their way, to walk before me in truth with all their heart and with all their soul, there shall not fail thee (said he) a man on the throne of Israel. Moreover thou knowest also what Joab the son of Zeruiah did to me, and what he did to the two captains of the hosts of Israel."

The "moreover" marks a moment when the nature of Solomon's attention would change. In the way of texts that accumulate meaning over centuries of layering, the anachronistic passage lets us imagine it as a mere interpolation, or as an overarching spiritual component of David's career, or as the old king's heed to convention, as lip service or with conviction. In any case, he gets to the urgent matter of killing old Joab.

Nor has David forgotten the cursing, stone-throwing

monkey of a man who threw epithets at the king when David was forced to leave Jerusalem:

"And behold, thou hast with thee Shimei the son of Gera, a Benjamite of Bahurim, which cursed me with a grievous curse in the day when I went to Mahanaim: but he came down to meet me at Jordan, and I sware to him by the Lord, saying, I will not put thee to death with the sword. Now therefore hold him not guiltless: for thou art a wise man, and knowest what thou oughtest to do unto him; but his hoar head bring thou down to the grave with blood."

The same awful concluding formula as for Joab, varied a little to be even more explicit. The dying man's vindictive demand for gray-haired Shimei to have a bloody end makes the more impressive David's restraint years earlier, when it was more politic to spare the ineffectual spitter of insults. And the restraint itself appears the more clearly to have less to do with mercy than with cool, mafioso calculation.

Then David dies, and is buried in the city of David, but his will, through Solomon, continues. Also David's ways: though David has not mentioned the priest Abiathar, who sided with Adonijah's party, Solomon summons him, dismisses him from his priesthood and spares him in the name of David, and in the manner of David. Solomon tells Abiathar:

"Get thee to Anathoth, unto thine own fields; for thou art worthy of death, but I will not at this time put thee to death, because thou barest the ark of the Lord God before David my father, and because thou hast been afflicted in all wherein my father was afflicted."

Shimei and Joab remain. Like David, Solomon shows some

mercy to the monkey-like hurler of epithets and rocks, then of abject apologies. Solomon tells Shimei to build a house for himself in Jerusalem, and not to leave the city again ever, on pain of death. As with David, Shimei contritely thanks the king and praises him. And as Solomon conceivably could anticipate, after three years in his Jerusalem house Shimei goes out on an expedition to Gath, pursuing a couple of runaway slaves. Thus Solomon like David before him gets another chance at Shimei, and can remind the man how effusively thankful he was for the arrangement he has violated. Solomon, again invoking David's name as he invoked it to Abiathar the priest, says to Shimei:

"Thou knowest all the wickedness which thine heart is privy to, that thou didst to David my father; therefore the Lord shall return thy wickedness upon thine own head. And king Solomon shall be blessed, and the throne of David shall be established before the Lord for ever. So the king commanded Benaiah the son of Jehoiada; which went out, and fell upon him, that he died."

And Joab, that long-serving and wily general, the murderer of Abner and Amasa, who first conspires with Absalom and then executes Absalom—Joab, though he may have outwitted himself in the end, is no fool. When he hears that Abiathar has been expelled from the priesthood and banished to Anathoth on pain of death, Joab runs for refuge. The once-powerful commander takes the same desperate course as Adonijah:

"And Joab fled unto the tabernacle of the Lord, and caught hold of the horns of the altar. And it was told king

Solomon that Joab was fled unto the tabernacle of the Lord; and behold, he is by the altar. Then Solomon sent Benaiah the son of Jehoiada, saying, Go, fall upon him."

Here is the old commander gripping the horns of the altar. And here is the young King Solomon, issuing orders to Benaiah. The king, like his father David, is aware of being watched by the nation. So Solomon's struggle of wills with the adamant old killer and conniver and protector Joab takes its course:

"And Benaiah came to the tabernacle of the Lord, and said unto him, Thus saith the king, Come forth. And he said, Nay; but I will die here. And Benaiah brought the king word again, saying, Thus said Joab, and thus he answered me. And the king said unto him, Do as he hath said, and fall upon him, and bury him; that thou mayest take away the innocent blood, which Joab shed, away from me, and from the house of my father."

So Benaiah, Joab's successor as strongman, kills him in the tabernacle. And Solomon, in more detail than with the priest Abiathar or with the jabbering Shimei, explains Joab's fate as part of the destiny of David. Solomon's words are explicit and oratorical, a kind of dynastic and patriotic poem:

"And the Lord shall return his blood upon his own head, who fell upon two men more righteous and better than he, and slew them with the sword, my father David not knowing thereof, to wit, Abner the son of Ner, captain of the host of Israel, and Amasa the son of Jether, captain of the host of Judah. Their blood shall therefore return upon the head of

Joab, and upon the head of his seed forever: but upon David and upon his seed, and upon his house, and upon his throne, shall there be peace for ever from the Lord."

The ends of little Shimei and great Joab manifest David's will, reaching beyond his death. But the end of Adonijah manifests David's enduring magnetism. The episode also demonstrates the character of Solomon. After David dies, Adonijah comes to Bathsheba with an extraordinary request. He has already bowed to the king his younger brother, and he has already been told, "Go to thine house."

Now, with David dead—apparently the moment that David is dead, and while Shimei and Joab are still alive, and Abiathar is still the priest—Adonijah comes from his house with a desire that continues the story of David's life in the imaginations and souls of his sons, and of his wife Bath-sheba, and indeed through them in the life of the kingdom:

"And Adonijah the son of Haggith came to Bathsheba the mother of Solomon. And she said, Comest thou peaceably? And he said, Peaceably. He said moreover, I have somewhat to say unto thee. And she said, Say on. And he said, Thou knowest that the kingdom was mine, and that all Israel set their faces on me, that I should reign: howbeit the kingdom is turned about, and is become my brother's: for it was his from the Lord."

The tentative, circling cadences of the dialogue, a pre-liminary fencing between Bathsheba and Adonijah, the handsome elder brother of King Solomon, has an intimate, naturalistic quality, far different from stylized formulas about hoar heads and enduring dynasties. Adonijah may be unable to resist alluding to how close he came to being king. "I have something to say unto thee," he says. His request, toward which he and Bathsheba sidle, may be a covert political bid. It may somehow be a gesture like Abner going in to the concubines of Saul, humiliating the weakling heir Ishbosheth, or like Absalom going in to the concubines of David, on the advice of the serpentine wise man Achitophel. Or, it may be sexual: a passion intricately related to all the submerged and tortuous fraternal and filial emotions that permeate the family of David, radiating from David. In any case, what the elder brother finally gets around to requesting from Bathsheba (is "stepmother" a term appropriate to polygamous families?) is bizarre:

"And now I ask one petition of thee," says Adonijah to Bathsheba—still inching his way toward it—"deny me not."

"And she said to him, Say on. And he said, Speak, I pray thee, unto Solomon the king, (for he will not say thee nay) that he give me Abishag the Shunamite to wife."

Sons of David seem destined repeatedly to try, one way or another, to become David. The form it takes here, if that hopeless emulation is even one meaning of Adonijah's petition to Bathsheba, is startling beyond measure. Bathsheba's answer is calm, or at least understated:

"And Bathsheba said, Well; I will speak for thee unto the king."

The next passage presents a revealing view of Bathsheba's place in Solomon's reign, and somehow this too, like Adonijah's petition, is a shadowy extension of the life of David:

"Bathsheba therefore went unto king Solomon, to speak

unto him for Adonijah. And the king rose up to meet her, and bowed himself unto her, and sat down on his throne, and caused a seat to be set for the king's mother; and she sat on his right hand."

In a film scene, Solomon's bow and Bathsheba's seat at his right would indicate her power, possibly her power over the king. But on the contrary, when Bathsheba makes the request on Adonijah's behalf—whether in sincere good faith or calculating that Adonijah is done for—though she sits at Solomon's right hand his mother receives from him not only a refusal but something like an ironic rebuke:

"And king Solomon answered and said unto his mother, And why dost thou ask Abishag the Shunamite for Adonijah? ask for him the kingdom also; for he is mine elder brother; even for him, and for Abiathar the priest, and for Joab the son of Zeruiah."

Solomon's outrage is not so much righteous as practical, the voice of brute common sense affronted. The notion of Adonijah having Abishag, who ministered to David, is for Solomon tantamount to giving the kingdom to his enemies— not just to Adonijah, but to the priest Abiathar and the not-yet-seen-to general Joab as well. And Solomon, who unlike Absalom and Adonijah has made no display of chariots with fifty men running before to show his regal importance, shows here a perhaps ruthless and certainly regal steel in his soul:

"Then king Solomon sware by the Lord, saying, God do so to me, and more also, if Adonijah have not spoken this word against his own life. Now therefore, as the Lord liveth, which hath established me, and set me on the throne of

David my father, and who hath made me an house, as he promised, Adonijah shall be put to death this day. And king Solomon sent by the hand of Benaiah the son of Jehoiada; and he fell upon him that he died."

With these executions King Solomon concludes in some respects the story of the life of David his father. In other respects, Solomon's alliance with the Pharaoh of Egypt, marrying his daughter; his building of the temple with the craftsmen of King Hiram of Tyre; his request to the Lord for wisdom and the Lord's rewarding of the request with not only wisdom but riches and success; Solomon's many wives and even his ambiguous following of their foreign gods— all echo David, as other sons of David could not do. The extended, obsessively detailed description of the Temple and its construction, embodying a perfect dream of a dynasty-founder's wish for his descendant, is like the Lord's ultimate love poem to David, through the accomplishment of the perfect heir, Solomon.

An Islamic legend tells that David's funeral dirge was chanted by forty thousand priests, but the account in the Book of Kings says only that he slept with his fathers and that he was buried in the City of David, having reigned forty years: seven in Hebron and thirty-three in Jerusalem. A tremendous, uncanny melancholy, and some truth about attained power, arise from the fact that his last recorded words are instructions to send his gray-haired enemy violently down to Sheol. As though bloodthirsty vendetta were doomed to be the final act in the drama of an irresistible boy, who sings to the harp to soothe a troubled king.

Psalm 110, identified as "A Psalm of David," encompasses the fresh promise of youth and the paranoia of experience in high office. Christians read it as David celebrating the future Jesus and Jews read it as a promise of the future messiah, but as a coronation song it has the worldly immediacy and the spiritual longing of the character David, himself.

This is a poem one can believe was written by David, as a vision of his own life. Though the Oxford Bible editors say, "The Hebrew text is unusually corrupt and the interpretation of many details extremely difficult," the violence and beauty of the man are clear enough. Even the marbling of opacity evokes the mysteries of David's character, a blur of withholding among the cruelty and sweetness. The poem begins:

> The Lord said unto my Lord, Sit thou at my right
> hand,
> until I make thine enemies thy footstool.
> The Lord shall send the rod of thy strength out of
> Zion:
> rule thou in the midst of thine enemies.
>
> Thy people shall be willing in the day of thy power
> in the beauties of holiness
> from the womb of the morning:
> thou hast the dew of thy youth.

Kingly rule in these lines is reconciled with the freshness and optimism of life's beginnings. The second half of the poem courts reassurance of divine favor. (Melchizedek is the ancient priest and king who blessed Abraham and received tithes from him: a figure of the most ancient authority and legitimacy, and so perhaps the healing or compensating opposite of an upstart.) The violence and desire for mastery are undiluted, as emphatic as David's words about Shimei and Joab. The poem concludes with a vision of slaking comfort at last:

> The Lord hath sworn, and will not repent,
> Thou art a priest for ever after the order of
>   Melchizedek.
> The Lord at thy right hand shall strike through kings
>   in the day of his wrath.
> He shall judge among the heathen,
>
> he shall fill the places with the dead bodies;
> he shall wound the heads over many countries.
> He shall drink of the brook in the way:
> therefore shall he lift up the head.

XII

David in Paradise

There is a Christian tradition of understanding David of Bethlehem as a foreshadowing or typification of Jesus. But on the other hand or equally David can be understood as rendering Jesus a tremendous afterthought, a precluded and showy iteration of David.

Louis Ginzberg's monumental *Legends of the Jews* retells the midrash account of judgment day, when God will prepare a banquet in Paradise for the souls of all the righteous. At the end of that glorious meal, "God will pass the wine cup over which grace is said, to Abraham, with the words: 'Pronounce the blessing over the wine, thou who art the father of the pious of the world.'" And Abraham will reply to the Lord that he is not worthy, because he is the father also of the Ishmaelites. God will turn then to Isaac, and ask him to recite the blessing instead, but Isaac will protest that he is unworthy, "for the children of my son Esau destroyed the temple." Then God invites Jacob, who will decline the honor because he too is unfit, since he was married to two sisters at once, which the Torah (albeit later) forbids. So the

Lord of Hosts will offer the cup to Moses: "Say the blessing, for thou didst receive the law and didst fulfill its precepts." And Moses will answer that since he was not worthy to enter the Holy Land surely he is not worthy to pronounce the blessing. Next, God will offer the blessing of the wine of the meal of the day of judgment to Joshua, the leader who brought the children of Israel to the Promised Land. And Joshua will say that he cannot be worthy of the honor because he was not found worthy to bring forth a son.

And at last, in the words of Ginzberg's great compilation, God will turn to David: "Take the cup and say the blessing, thou the sweetest singer in Israel and Israel's king." And David will reply:

"Yes, I will pronounce the blessing, for I am worthy of the honor."

This may be an account less of David's arrogance than of his unmitigated fitness beyond *chutzpah* and above challenge—and possibly a matter less of fitness pure and sanctified than of David's particular and personally fitting destiny: the resistless outcome of character, structured like a Jewish joke but with a punchline of outrageous, transcendent and insuperably cockeyed redemption:

"Then God will take the Torah and read various passages from it, and David will recite a psalm in which both the pious in Paradise and the wicked in hell will join with a loud Amen. Thereupon God will send his angels to lead the wicked from hell to Paradise."

AFTERWORD

I have quoted the Hebrew Bible mainly from the King James translation and its offspring, because I write in English, and not only is the King James regarded on its merits as the greatest translation into English ever, of anything; it also echoes through memorable writing in our tongue, with endless variety—in the cadences and vocabulary and images and fabular allusions of Dickens and Dickinson, of Keats and Whitman, of Pope and Faulkner, of Melville and Ellison, of Lincoln and Churchill, of Flannery O'Connor and Allen Ginsberg.

And as a great work lives through its followers and descendants, enduring by changing, so too does a great character live through successive generations and centuries of different apprehensions. Memory is a work of imagination. The story of a figure like David becomes inevitably a story of stories. A life of such dimension becomes also the life of its retellings, staged on excavated pavilions of darkness and light.

But I have tried not to let English make David too familiar or easily recognizable, a modern or Jacobean ruler in biblical dress. Jewish legend and interpretation obviate any notion of a merely King James or Christianized David—an "Old Testament" David as a friend of mine has put it—become like the fallen Temple depicted on cathedral walls, a mere precursor of the successful offshoot religion, the Christianity that saw Jews as having hung up their harps and never taken them down again. English is after all a profoundly Christianized language, with for example "spirit" an abstract Latin term carrying little of its root as "breath" when it translates Hebrew *ruach*, the word used for a current in water or a breeze in air.

David is more enigmatic than any purely Christian or Jewish paradigm: more tangled at the roots, and more proliferating, larger. An enduring story of stories necessarily involves quirks and guises, a paradoxical encrustation of midrash. For example, the six-pointed figure known as the Star of David (or Shield of David) was pretty certainly unknown to David. Although Gregory Peck wears the image on his tunic in *David and Bathsheba*, the six-pointed star was not associated with King David, nor with Jews, until more than a thousand years after the time of David.

The star is of David, the Psalms are of David, the very stories in the Hebrew Bible and in the legends are of David: all are *of* him by sovereign, possessive force of attribution beyond scholarly demonstration—in their different ways and degrees all rotating around David's genitive, central energy that attracts and embraces them.

In the Roman Forum, on the triumphal arch of the Emperor Titus, celebrating his capture and destruction of Jerusalem a millennium after its founding, the branched candelabrum appears, but not the anachronistic star. It is not mentioned in the Bible, nor in the Talmud, nor in the rabbinical literature. The first Jewish source to mention the star is in the thirteenth century of the Common Era, and the symbol does not appear to be much used before the fifteenth century. The *Jewish Encyclopedia* says of the star, "It is probable that it was the Cabala that derived the symbol from the Templars." The Knights Templar, the Cabala—this genealogy of the figure resembles the texture of arcana in a genre novel.

In the course of time it has become not merely accepted but central. Moreover, the figure embraces symbolically its own history of adaptation and flux. In a traditional iconography, the two triangles represent an accepting dual embrace of heaven above and the earth below, in the interwoven yin and yang: the male blade pointing upward opens wide to embrace the earth, while the female chalice pointing earthward opens wide to embrace heaven. Exceeding the five fingers of that other Cabalistic motif the hand, the Mogen David like the son of Jesse comes from outside to become central and inclusive. It is a symbol, among other things, of including whatever is in heaven or on earth.

The Star of David's history has been far from uniformly sweet. When the Portuguese monarch Affonso IV (1325–57) reversed his predecessors' benign policies, all Jews were forbidden to appear in public without wearing a visible, six-pointed yellow star on their hat or coat. (In this regard the Nazis again appear as not originators but copiers, adapters, exploiters and refiners.) Continuing and extending the theme of inclusion, Gerschom Scholem in his essay on the star commends the wisdom of converting the symbol of oppression into an insignia of national identity. On the flag of Israel, and as a glyph unmistakable as the cross, the stringent geometry of the star in the way of human makings accepts but transfigures its range of meanings.

Here is a particular instance: a photograph of twelve young men, taken in the bad year 1939. Sewn onto their uniforms is that six-pointed star of interlocked triangles, said to be borrowed from a device of the Knights Templar and incorporated without rabbinic approval into the agonized mysticisms and pedantries of Cabala. The young men squinting back at the camera are named Ralph Binder, Joseph Siegel, Nathan Schneider, Morris Newberg, Herman Schneider, Gilbert Kaplan, Harry Silver, David Becker, Milton Silver, Milford Pinsky, Abraham Baum and Seymour Barron.

They are the Jewish Aces, in shorts, kneepads and basketball shoes. One of them holds a basketball on which someone has painted: "City Champs, 1938–39." Another cradles the trophy, with its crowning figure of an athlete holding the ball overhead in the trophy-maker's stylized gesture of attainment, in plated metal. They are standing in front of their high school in Long Branch, New Jersey.

1939! The group picture is an interesting artifact because of the apparent, wacky or tragic incongruity of that six-pointed emblem, deployed in Europe for such different purposes—far more like those of King Affonso—at the moment the photograph was taken. The players of the Jewish Aces were most likely far from unaware of the laws and measures enacted by the Third Reich. Some of them would eventually go into battle against that regime. It seems safe to assume also that on that sunny afternoon in Long Branch, beaming at the camera, the young men were aware of the assertive, maybe even defiant quality of the team's name: The Jewish Aces. The implications of "Aces"—superior, raffish, primary, sensual, worldly, singular or lone, victorious, adept—also fit David.

In such impure, fluid, partly accidental manifestations, certain human doings continue as nodes of energy: durably complex particles that radiate, shift and recombine to exceed likelihood, and evade prediction. King David, like the six-pointed design he would not have recognized, gathers meaning in a systole and diastole of need and invention—over centuries of attainment and outrage, suffering and ordinary life, in an endlessly glamorous, stubborn accretion.

A READER'S GUIDE

In *The Life of David*, Robert Pinsky brings the biblical figure of David to life, teasing apart the many strands of his story—leader, outlaw, poet, warrior, son, father, lover—and then weaving them together into a vibrant biography of this most celebrated biblical king. The following questions are ways to begin exploring some of these threads.

Artist and Artistry

1. David is most often remembered as a warrior and king, but, like Robert Pinsky, he is also a poet, named by the Bible as the author of many of the psalms. How does this change our image of David? What aspects of his character are learned from the psalms Pinsky uses to illustrate the story? How might Pinsky's life as a poet color his retelling?

2. Pinsky writes, "The hero requires the artist who celebrates him." Why do you think so many artists over time—Michelangelo, Donatello, Rembrandt, British playwrights George Peele and John Dryden—have been drawn to David as a subject?

3. How is our image of David influenced by depictions of him in Christian art such as the detail from the Sistine Chapel that appears on the jacket?

4. How does language affect the telling of this story? Pinsky's preference is for the anglicized names of people and places and the King James Version. Would readers relate differently to the story if the characters were known by Hebrew transliterations of their names—Avshalom, Batsheva, Shlomo, Shaul—and if the English text was drawn from a contemporary translation?

Leadership

1. David's reign as king reveals his strength of character as well as his flaws. How does David shed light on the biblical ideal of leadership?

2. Pinsky writes, "A hero is one who does great deeds and suffers for the good of the community." While David's deeds are indisputably great, does David suffer for the community? What are the causes of David's troubles?

3. What qualities of leadership do David and Saul share?

4. David makes many mistakes in his reign but is always forgiven by God, who chose him and who continues to promise him an eternal throne. Why is he forgiven and Saul rejected?

Fathers, Sons, Brothers, and Heirs

1. Like so many biblical heroes—Isaac, Jacob, Moses—David is the younger son who is elevated over his older brothers. What does the Bible suggest by repeatedly inverting the traditional order?

2. Fathers and sons are a recurring motif in this story: Saul fears David, his son-in-law, will turn his son Jonathan against him; David is undermined in various ways by his sons Amnon, Absalom, and Adonijah. How do David's own actions—and inaction—contribute to the dysfunction of his family?

3. When the young David comes to fight Goliath, he is given Saul's armor but, overburdened by its weight, removes it. However, he has no trouble wearing Jonathan's garments and shield, given to him as a symbol of love. What does this reveal about the relationships among these three men?

4. How is Saul's donning a disguise to see the Witch of Endor different from what Pinsky refers to as David's "shape-shifting"?

David in Love

1. The Bible so often leaves the women unrecorded, yet David's story is filled with women, from his great-grandmother Ruth to his wives—Michal, Abigail, Bathsheba—to his daughter, Tamar. What do these women teach David? What do his interactions with them reveal about his character?

2. How are the women in this story used as symbols of male power? Who among them manages to assert her own authority? Who fails to do so?

3. In another birth-order inversion, David marries Saul's younger daughter, Michal, who loves him, instead of the older daughter, Merab. Is Michal's role in their relationship a departure from the roles of women in the Bible?

4. What went wrong between Michal and David? Are love and hate always as closely entwined as Pinsky makes them out to be in this story?

5. "Therefore Michal the daughter of Saul had no child unto the day of her death." Is Michal childless as a consequence of the never-healed rift between her and David, or as a divine punishment for her disdain for his joyful dance of worship before the Ark?

Divine Justice and Human Vengeance

1. Both David and Saul employ a code of justice and vengeance that seems grounded in the biblical command of "an eye for an eye"—a system that the rabbis of the Mishnah, 1,000 years later, repudiated in favor of a system of paid damages. Why do these leaders so ruthlessly adhere to this often brutal code?

2. Divine justice, too, often functions in these stories as a calculated exchange, a system that is not limited to God's prophets but is also the language of the magicians and divines of the surrounding Gentile cultures. How is this different from contemporary ideas about justice?

3. When David sleeps with Bathsheba and then has her husband killed, he confesses and throws himself on God's mercy in a psalm that has become the core of Jewish penitential prayer. Why does he insist that his sin is against God alone and ignore his victim? Is his confession sufficient?

God's Choosing

1. David, whose name means "beloved," is chosen to be king of the Israelites after the first divinely chosen king, Saul, is rejected by God. What does the divine need to change and reassess the choice reveal about God?

2. David relates to God through the calculus of divine justice but also through a joyful spirit of celebration, seen when he dances exultingly before the Ark of God and when he prophesizes in Ramah. Yet Saul is mocked when he joins these same dancing prophets. Why does this behavior seem natural for David but alien, and even ridiculous, in Saul?

3. Why does God decline David's offer to build the Temple? According to Jewish tradition, the blood of war on David's hands made him unfit to build the house of God. Yet Solomon, who is permitted to build the Temple, himself wages war and kills his brother. Why might God prefer that Solomon perform this task?

David the Myth

1. Of the many great stories of David's life—David and Goliath, David and Bathsheba, David and Saul, David and Jonathan, David and Absalom, to list but a few—which are the most familiar? What parts of David's story came as a surprise to you?

2. In Jewish liturgy the Messiah is often referred to as "the seed of David" or "the house of David." Why is David, rather than Moses or Abraham, the eternal leader of the Jewish people?

3. How do David and the stories of his life continue to figure into Jewish discourse as symbols of the endurance of the Jewish people and, since its establishment in 1948, as symbols of the State of Israel?

4. Christian theology claims that David's kingship is a prefiguration of Jesus. Pinsky recounts a midrash, a rabbinic story that attempts to illuminate the biblical text, in which David is shown to be the greatest of all the biblical heroes and leaders of the Jewish people. How does this explain Pinsky's point that "David can be understood as rendering Jesus an afterthought, a precluded and showy iteration of David?"

5. Why might the religions that honor David—Judaism, Christianity, and Islam—emphasize some stories and not others?

ABOUT THE AUTHOR

Robert Pinsky is the author of many books of poetry, including *Jersey Rain* and *The Figured Wheel*, and of the award-winning translation *The Inferno of Dante*. His prose works include *The Situation of Poetry* and *The Sounds of Poetry*. He teaches in the graduate creative writing program at Boston University and lives in Massachusetts.